# THE LIFE ENERGY IN MUSIC: NOTES ON MUSIC AND SOUND

## VOLUME I

JOHN DIAMOND, M.D.

For additional writings on music by John Diamond refer to:

- *YOUR BODY DOESN'T LIE*, Warner Books, New York, 1980.
- *SPEECH, LANGUAGE AND THE POWER OF THE BREATH*, Valley Cottage, 1979.
- *THE COLLECTED PAPERS OF JOHN DIAMOND, M.D., VOLUME II*, Valley Cottage, 1980.
- *LIFE ENERGY: Understanding and Transforming Your Emotions to Achieve Total Health*, A & W, New York, 1983.
- *THE LIFE ENERGY IN MUSIC, VOLUME II*, Valley Cottage, 1983.

All available from Archaeus Press

**THE LIFE ENERGY IN MUSIC:
NOTES ON MUSIC AND SOUND**

**VOLUME I**

Published by the Archaeus Press
Post Office Drawer 37
Valley Cottage, NY 10989


Second Printing 1983

## CONTENTS

## DEDICATION

This is my tribute to Music, my inadequate attempt to express gratitude to Her for all that She has done for me. In particular, for all the years that She has comforted and sustained me.

I wish to thank all the musicians with whom I have had the privilege to work over the years, especially John Buttrick.

And most of all, my sincere gratitude to all the great composers and musicians who have given us so much from their hearts over the years.

*"There is in souls a sympathy with sounds, . . .*
*Some chord in unison with what we hear*
*Is touch'd within us, and the heart replies."*

*– Cowper*

*"Music is love."*

*– Hanslick*

*"Music is the art of the prophets, the only art that can calm the agitations of the soul; it is one of the most magnificent and delightful presents God has given us."*

*– Luther*

## PREFACE

This is a series of papers reporting findings in some of the many areas of research in progress at the Institutes for the Enhancement of Life Energy and Creativity on the effects of music and sound.

As it is about music I have tried to be musical. I have not tried to write a scientific, logical, dry treatise directed to your already overworked analytical left brain. I have instead directed my work to your whole brain. I have tried to use rhythms and gestures and patterns of flow which I hope may be somewhat more helpful to you as a total experience than the reading of yet another fact-filled book. There are passages which you may feel are repetitious or in which the logic may appear convoluted and rambling. Of course, some of these are my faults of logic and style, but many times they are my attempts to activate your right brain by using particular patterns.

I wish I were a competent musician. Unfortunately I am not, and this must be my substitute. Just as music does not come to life until it is performed, you will find that you will derive the greatest understanding from what I have written if you read it aloud.

# INTRODUCTION

Recently I attended a performance of a chamber music concert. A famous violinist led the performances, which included a violin-piano sonata and a work for string ensemble. The New York Times had given the concert a rave review; the audience applauded and cheered. But it was easy to see that only two musicians were involved in the musical pulse and able to give themselves over to it. Mostly we were seeing a series of virtuoso tasks and plain hard work. Visible physical tensions, lack of respiration, and anguished facial contortions were further distress signals. And so, once again, we missed the Dionysian joy, the ecstasy, the lithe and elastic physical movement that is music's unique gift.

Many of us in the profession have noted the current state of affairs and have been unable to see a way to effect alternatives. Yet the haunting knowledge remains: our musical ideal often remains locked in us at the point of performance, and we seldom derive the pleasure of passing it on to a listener. We can see and hear this frustration in the orchestral musician's playing and the self-aggrandizing movements of the modern conductor. We are sold records of those groups by companies whose fanaticism with fidelity completely ignores the point of it all – to transmit that elusive heart and breath of the unstressed contact point between composer and performer. Anyone who has seen the inside of a recording studio, which looks more like an intensive care unit, knows that it is unlikely to produce a worthy result.

Three years ago my career was progressing nicely – from the public point of view. More tours with two world famous string quartets were in the offing, my latest record had been well received, my new excellent European manager was going to arrange additional tours there on my behalf, and there were soon to be more records. I had a waiting list of students. My concertizing was at an all-time high and the reviews were most laudatory. But there was too often a lack of inner pleasure with making music. Performances were surrounded with doubts about certain difficult passages, or the possibility of losing a movement's musical thread, or what the critics might say. Practicing was often compulsive and physically stressful. Worst of all, I didn't really enjoy music.

Around that time a friend took me to a seminar given by John Diamond. After the first flush of astonishment at how incisive and revealing the deltoid muscle testing really was, I soon was understanding that here was a way, an art, which could reach farther into my stress points, my often dormant creative life, and my faltering capacity to give out, than I had believed possible.

Previous assistance from psychiatry, the Alexander Technique, exercise programs, and careful nutrition had helped but had simply slowed up a general wave of musical and/psychic stress. From the very start of the work with John Diamond I had the sense of renewing or re-focusing attitudes and feeling immediate effects on my physical and inner life. The depth of creative experience that was unlocked when the ego was dispatched to its proper niche was as gratifying as anything I had experienced. And, as time passed, I had a feeling that at last the proper instrument was being tuned, with the newly found resonance enhancing many areas of life.

I know now that my playing has the capacity to physically strengthen people. And there are moments when suddenly I am aware that the audience and I are breathing together, that I am simply the prism through which all of this flows. The biological imperative of rhythmic pulse and expansion of musical motifs has replaced studied effects. Physical stress in difficult passages has been reduced; the overriding power of proper breathing and more constructive attitudes have seen to that.

The real substance of all this work, though, is that the love of music which was mine as a youth is present in my playing and contemplation of music. The technical discipline and musical artfulness acquired in study and teaching is its balance wheel, not its controllant. Yet there is no conscious sense of having arrived at a magical point of assured success. Rather, the old ice-bound rivulets of scattered musical life have come together and channeled into a broad, expansive river. The water is fresher, the light iridescent, the current steady even through some rapids. As I go on and with this flow, music is no longer just a profession, it is an instrument of my aspiration.

John Buttrick
Professor of Music
Massachusetts Institute
of Technology

January 1981

# THE HEALING POWER OF MUSIC

I honor music as a true and great therapy that activates the life energy within each individual. Hippocrates called this the Vis Medicatrix Naturae – the Healing Power of Nature. Paracelsus spoke of it as the Archaeus. It is Prana, Chi, Spirit. It evokes the true and only healing, that which occurs from within.

A drug may relieve the symptoms of a disease but it does not cure. The true cure always involves a major change in the patient's attitude to himself, to life, and to God. The cure ultimately must be in the soul.

Of all the physical modalities, music most activates the life energy and uplifts the soul. Only pure love can do more.

Simple deltoid muscle testing will show that most people test weak looking at a fluorescent light or thinking of an unpleasant situation or in response to any other form of stress.* It will be found that when music is played they will now test strong in the presence of the same stressful stimulus. The music has made them invulnerable to the stress.

It will also be found on test that 95% of the population will have low thymus activity + – and thus low life energy as the thymus is a master controller of the life energy. The thymus activity will instantly be raised by listening to music.

The basic therapeutic activity of music is the raising of life energy, reducing the effects of all stresses and noxious stimuli and enhancing the healing powers within.

---

* YOUR BODY DOESN'T LIE, John Diamond, M.D., Warner Books, New York, 1980, p. 63.

+ Ibid., p. 84. Also refer to Appendix II.

# THE LIFE ENERGY OF MUSIC AND PERFORMANCE

*"Music, throughout its long history, has been thought of or used as a healing agent."**

The basic purpose of music is to be therapeutic, to raise the life energy of the listener. This simple yet profound truth seems to have been forgotten in this era which acclaims technical virtuosity and sophisticated musicology. The function of music since its beginning has been the spiritual uplifting of the listener so that his life energy is enhanced by the experience.

Thus it is that over the centuries music has been considered one of the great therapies. For example, this was realized and implemented by Pythagoras. And we read in the Odyssey that Odysseus' companions "bandaged the wound, staying the dark blood with a song of healing." It is implicit in the writings of many of the great doctors

*"Music, Physician of the Soul," Emanuel Winternitz.

throughout the ages, such as Caelius Aurelianus and Moses Maimonides, who gave very precise instructions for its medicinal uses. None of us is surprised to read that music was employed by David to soothe Saul. We all realize that music has that power. Yet we overlook this when we play it, when we go to a concert or when we choose a record. We have forgotten the very reason for music's existence.

— — —

The genesis of all communication is in the baby's earliest relationship with his mother, especially her voice, and that voice sings to him. Music starts with the lullaby and all the beautiful lilting sounds that the mother makes to the baby. It is a vehicle of love that overcomes all stresses and discomforts. Just listen to a mother comforting her crying infant with her smiling and her rocking and her lilting music, and you cannot help but realize that this must be the basis of all communication. It is love and comfort, reducing the stress and raising the life energy.

We are led to the inevitable conclusion that something has gone wrong with our appreciation of music. We do not hear a critic say that he was uplifted or benefitted by a performance. We are all obsessed instead with the technique and other superficial criteria which have little to do with the real purpose of music. A mother singing out of key will do more for her baby than a cold-hearted coloratura soprano.

For over twenty-five years in my practice, I have been researching what it is in music that has this life-enhancing quality and how it can best be used as therapy. For example, I have found that it can be used as analgesia for relief of pain and even as anesthesia for some surgical procedures – there is an ancient Greek motto, "Men have song as a physician for pain." I use it for overcoming all emotional imbalances, anxieties, phobias, depression, even acute psychosis. Of course it relieves insomnia – this was after all the reason for Bach's composing the Goldberg Variations. I have used it in programs for withdrawal from addictive drugs. And more fundamentally, whenever I wish to activate the patient's will to be well and his life energy. The uses are endless – in fact, it is an integral part of my daily practice. The more I use music, the more I realize how little I know about what it can really do. There seems to be no instance in which the correct music cannot be of major benefit.

Just recently I was called to the hospital to see a friend who had an operation the previous day. When I arrived he was in much pain and distress. His pulse was very fast, his respiration was shallow and from the upper chest with no apparent diaphragmatic excursion at all. His whole appearance was one of fear and pain. The first thing I did was to play the correct music. He heard this with his ears, but also I directed it with transducers to specific acupuncture points on his body which were related to the pain he was experiencing.* Within a minute

* For details of the procedure involved, refer to "Music for the Reduction of Pain" in this collection.

his pain had completely disappeared, he was breathing easily and now with obvious diaphragmatic excursion, his pulse had dropped from 116 to 70, he was smiling and he had a glow in his cheeks instead of the white pallor of fear. He sighed and relaxed and was then able to express to me how frightened he was of being in the hospital. Shortly afterward, he was up and walking. This is the power of music. And this has been known to the ancients and is still known among "primitive" societies today.

Probably in all cultures including our own, music has been used as part of medical treatment. For example, it was an integral function of the healing temples of Asklepios in ancient Greece. It is still part of the healing practices of nearly every "primitive" tribe. Chanting and dancing are essential features of the work of the medicine man and the shaman. But today music is completely divorced from our Western medicine. It has been replaced by the clatter of stainless steel in the hospital corridors and the din of the patients' television sets and the incessant intrusion of the paging system.

I frequently demonstrate to doctors a tape recording made at a patient's bedside in a modern American hospital and contrast that with a tape recording made in a Mexican hospital. There the predominant sound is of songbirds in the courtyard. From dawn till dark the patient hears not the sounds of our modern technological "advances" but the beautiful healing sounds of nature. When medicine abandoned music it lost its spirit.

But a remnant still exists. Music is still very much a part of all religious services – a recognition of its spiritual role. But again we do not consider this role when listening to and judging music in a concert hall. In fact, today some "sophisticated" churchgoers will comment on the technical quality of the music performed in the church; but fortunately the "unsophisticated" will describe it in spiritual terms and say how uplifted they were by it, how it opened their hearts and brought them closer to God. This I believe is the true purpose of music.

## *A NEW SYSTEM OF AESTHETICS*

I am proposing a system of aesthetics which has little to do with formal music training and theory and is not primarily concerned with technique. Although these are extremely important factors, they must never take first place. I am proposing a system of musical judgment and appreciation which concerns itself with the basics of music, not with superficialities. A system which asks and answers the questions, "Does this music raise our life energy? Has mankind benefitted by the performance?"

Over the years we at the Institutes for the Enhancement of Life Energy and Creativity have tested some 25,000 recordings of Western classical and popular music as well as the ethnic music of many cultures. Using specific testing on listeners, we have been able to delineate the degree of life energy enhancing qualities of most composers, and even the changes of energy as their musical lives progress. We can also delineate the precise degree of life energy enhancing qualities of the performers on all instruments as well as singers and conductors.

The test is a purely objective test. There is nothing subjective about it. For the first time criticism is taken out of the realm of "I like it" or "I don't like it" or "It makes me feel good." This tests what it does physiologically.

To arrive at the conclusions requires sophisticated testing far beyond the scope of this paper. In this preliminary communication I intend to restrict myself to one simple test which you can easily perform for yourself. This has to do with the study of the breathing of the listener. With this test you will be able to delineate two groups of performers – those who are stressed and those who are not stressed by the act of performing.

## *THE RESPIRATORY ENERGY SPONTANEOUS PULSATION*

Before describing the test let us consider the following: For many years I have played to students the same passage of the same work by different performers. A typical example is the opening of the third movement of the Beethoven Ninth Symphony. If I play a Furtwangler performance, I will see almost within seconds that the entire group is breathing synchronously, all their chests seem to be moving in unison. When this is pointed out to them, they recognize the phenomenon. If next I play a low energy recording of the same passage, this uniform respiratory pulsation throughout the group does not materialize. Instead everyone seems to breathe at a different rate and in a shallow fashion. Many times when I have done this demonstration, members of the group will remark that they notice that their breathing has become shallow and irregular and that they are not breathing in unison. With the Furtwangler performance, they were all breathing to the Respiratory Energy Spontaneous Pulsation (RESP) * purely transmitted by Furtwangler. With the low energy performance, the RESP has been broken and distorted by the performer's stress which prevents him from identifying with Beethoven's pulse.

You will find the same at a concert. With a high energy performer nearly everyone in the audience will be breathing in unison, as if the entire concert hall, including the performer, is pulsating at one with the composer. The healing power of the music is in this pulse and thus these performances are healing experiences. Whether the members of the audience realize it or not, their energies have been raised and their stresses have been reduced.

On the other hand, if the performer is stressed, the breathing in concert does not take place and the full healing potential of the music will not be realized.

Here is a simple test you can do which will enable you to divide performers (but not composers) into two groups, those who can transmit the RESP and those who are too stressed to be able to do so. This obviously is not as sophisticated as the testing used in our research, but it is nonetheless highly valuable. It will give you an understanding of the real purpose of music and a new system by

* SPEECH, LANGUAGE AND THE POWER OF THE BREATH, John Diamond, Valley Cottage, 1979.

which you yourself can judge musical performance. Now you can make informed decisions concerning which performers you choose to hear. By today's standards we may say that any of the major concert artists have good technique. But there is something more which is irrespective of the technique. They must be unstressed by their performance, for only then can they give of their hearts. When this occurs, we will receive with the heart. The communication will be as with the mother, from heart to heart.* We may or may not be thrilled by the pyrotechnics and the loud climaxes. They soon fade. But if the heart is there, the music can live on inside us and we can grow.

## *THE LIFE ENERGY BREATH SPAN TEST*

This test is the Life Energy Breath Span Test (LEBST). Firstly, to familiarize yourself with the general deltoid muscle testing technique, begin by having the listener stand with his left arm straight out to his side, at right angles to his body, making sure that his elbow is perfectly straight.+ Then the tester, facing the subject, pushes down on the outstretched arm near the wrist with approximately eight to ten pounds of pressure with a firm, fairly swift action. The subject should be able to resist this pressure easily. There should be a spring in

---

* THE RE-MOTHERING EXPERIENCE, John Diamond, Valley Cottage, 1981.

+ refer to Appendix I and YOUR BODY DOESN'T LIE, p. 42.

his shoulder joint indicating the integrity of the deltoid muscle which we are testing.

Once the subject is accustomed to the standard testing technique, next ask him to take in a big breath and hold it* while the tester pushes on the outstretched arm at approximately two-second intervals to test whether the deltoid muscle is still capable of withstanding the stress while he is holding his breath. You will find that subjects differ markedly in the length of time elapsed before testing weak while holding the breath, an indication of the basic level of their life energy.

In the LEBST, we measure the length of time the subject can hold his breath and continue to have strength in the muscle while listening to various performances of the same passage of music. When you conduct this phase of the test, you will find that regardless of the length of time a subject could hold his breath without the music stimulus, he will tend to fall into one of two groups while listening to the test music. With some performers, the subject will be able to hold his breath for only a short time, such as five seconds, while with other performances of the same passage of music he will be able to hold his breath and still test strong for quite some time, even up to forty seconds.

Thus we can see that through the implementation of this test performers can easily be divided into two

---

* It does not matter at what point of the respiratory cycle he holds his breath, but as most people want to hold it at full inspiration we have standardized the test at that phase of respiration.

categories. Those whose music enabled the subject to hold his breath for a long time before testing weak are high energy, unstressed performers and their music thus enables the subject to reduce his own stress and increase his own life energy. Those performers whose music did not produce this result are stressed and have low energy levels while performing, and this is transmitted to the listener. The effect on the subject was irrespective of the subject's breath span length when no test music was played.*

As an example, a controlled double blind experiment was conducted using thirty subjects and testing the beginning of the first movement of five Beethoven piano sonatas. We tested commercial recordings as well as a few recordings of concert performances. A total of forty-six performers were tested in 128 different performances.

It was easy to differentiate the performers on the basis of the Life Energy Breath Span Test. They fell into two groups – the five-second group (the "stressed" performers) and the twenty-five second group (the "unstressed" performers). There were fifteen high energy (unstressed) performers and thirty-one stressed performers. Tragically, only six of the high energy performers are concertizing at this time. I do not wish to make reference

* By the very nature of this test it is difficult to be absolutely precise with the timing as the testing itself takes time. However, the two distinct groups are quite obvious. Further, those who held their breath for long periods with certain performances often stopped when they did because they felt they had run out of air – not because they were actually weak.

to any living performers in this paper,* but instead to point out the differences in performances that you can discover, and how these differences relate to the very basic purpose of music – its therapeutic effect.

– – – –

Obviously many factors must be considered and assessed when establishing performance criteria. The Life Energy Breath Span Test is offered as an alternative to the staid analytical academic approach in which technical virtuosity transcends heart. It is also offered as an alternative to those performance criteria which can be influenced by public taste and fashion. It recognizes that music is more than entertainment.

The LEBST relates to the physiology of music, to the effect on the body. It has little to do with technical virtuosity for its own sake. Of course without a high level of technique the composer's pulse cannot be transmitted, but the LEBST transcends considerations of technique. And being a physiological response, it is impervious to publicity hype. Furthermore, it tests what is most important in music – not its academic criteria,

* nor in this book, with one exception.

nor sentimental or superficial emotionalism. Rather it tests the very reason for the existence of music – it tests its therapeutic ability, its ability to heal us. We must not forget that music is the great therapy, and the transcendental performers* are the great therapists.

All the artists in the study cited are great virtuosi and all have a thorough knowledge of music. But something more is involved. They must be able to transmit the pulse of the composer. In the case of Beethoven this is a very high energy pulse,+ particularly in his later works. If the performer can transmit this, then we are healed by the experience and the performer becomes one of the descendants of a long line of musical heritage. These high energy musicians can comfort us, support us, elevate us, raise our spirit, and heal us – in the way that our mothers could, in the way of nature.

Interestingly, in all the recordings of performers we have tested, we find that they rarely change their energy levels as they progress through life. For example, recordings of Casals over a period of nearly fifty years reveal no change in his life energy. In some cases we have found performers whose life energy has diminished on their latest recordings – and we are not surprised when we soon read that they have become seriously ill or have died. But even so, it is rare in recordings made

---

* Only a very small minority of the high energy performers belong to this category. The testing procedure for this distinction is beyond the scope of this paper.

\+ refer to "Towards an Understanding of Beethoven: Some Preliminary Notes," in this collection.

even within a short time of the death of an artist to find a change in life energy. Pierre Monteux and Dinu Lipatti are two examples of this.

We have never found a performer whose energy improved over the years without therapeutic intervention. It seems that once he becomes a professional his stress level is set. It is here that major research of the Institutes for the Enhancement of Life Energy and Creativity and the Archaeus Research Foundation is being directed. We have had most gratifying results working with performers to reduce the stress of their performances and thus so raise their life energies that they are able to be totally at one with the pulse of the composer. They have been able to change from untherapeutic performers to transcendental performers.

## THE LEVELS OF THERAPEUTIC COMMUNICATION

We will begin by defining three levels of life energy:

1. **High thymus activity.** Those whose thymus energy tests strong*. These are people who at the time of testing have high life energy and are on the path of health. The will to be well is active. They tend to embrace the positive things in life and are dedicated to their own health and welfare as well as that of those around them. They have what we call the high thymus attributes – love, faith, gratitude, trust and courage. These people are much less vulnerable to life's stresses. There is a balance of activity between their two cerebral hemispheres and therefore they are creative. This type usually comprises about 5% of a sample population.

2. **Vulnerable to stress.** Most of the population will test weak for thymus activity. They have an inadequate supply of life energy. They are much more vulnerable

---

* see Appendix II.

to stress. There is cerebral hemisphere imbalance* and they are less creative. This comprises the majority of people.

3. **Umbilicus problem.** There is a small yet definite group who have what we call an "umbilicus problem." These people are more disease-prone. The umbilicus problem is an indication that the so-called "death instinct" is triumphant over the life instinct of the individual at that time.+

We are all aware that within us there are forces for health and forces for ill health. An obvious example is seen in a smoker. Each time he takes a puff it is the "death instinct" within him which is motivating him. Each time a person who is aware of the detrimental effects of junk food nevertheless chooses to eat it he is revealing the dominance of the "death instinct" at that time. Each time he chooses not to eat it this is a manifestation of the life instinct. There is constantly within us a battle between these two forces. Our behavior from moment to moment is influenced by this battle. In any given day we act a certain number of times in accordance with the "death instinct" and a certain number of times in accordance with the life instinct. When an individual

* YOUR BODY DOESN'T LIE, p. 65.

+ "The Umbilicus Problem," THE COLLECTED PAPERS OF JOHN DIAMOND, M.D., VOLUME II, Valley Cottage, 1980. Also THE REMOTHERING EXPERIENCE and Appendix III.

tests as having an umbilicus problem, at that time the death instinct is triumphant and thus he is actually predisposed to disease.

We have found that music falls into one of five major groups as regards the therapeutic power of its communication:

**Group I.** DECIDEDLY UNTHERAPEUTIC. These are musical communications which actually produce an umbilicus problem in the listener – that is, actually activate the "death instinct" within him. This occurs after prolonged exposure to certain rock music.*

**Group II.** UNTHERAPEUTIC. This music produces stress. It will cause a person whose thymus activity is testing strong to test weak when exposed to the music.+

**Group III.** NONTHERAPEUTIC or neutral. This group neither raises nor lowers the life energy. If the subject's thymus activity is testing weak, it will continue to test weak. If it was testing strong, it will continue to test strong. Electronically synthesized music and muzak belong to this group. There is no pulse at all – neither beneficial nor harmful.

**Group IV.** THERAPEUTIC. This group will raise the life energy of the listener. If his thymus gland was

* "What's Really Wrong with Rock Music," THE COLLECTED PAPERS OF JOHN DIAMOND, VOLUME II.

+ Appendix II and YOUR BODY DOESN'T LIE, p. 151.

previously testing weak, it will now test strong. The great body of music, popular and classical, falls into this class. There are many levels within this group from those which are barely therapeutic to those that are highly therapeutic.

**Group V.** TRANSCENDENTAL music. This is the highest energy group of all. Only this group can reverse the "death instinct." This is the music to use for all healing purposes. This is music that is divinely therapeutic.

## THE GENESIS OF MUSIC

*"In the germ, when the first trace of life begins to stir, music is the nurse of the soul; it murmurs in the ear, and the child sleeps; the tones are companions of his dreams – they are the world in which he lives."* – *Bettini*

A very fine musician and composer tells me that her earliest memories are of singing songs with her mother. These memories go back to before she was two years old. She also says that her family tells her that from the day she was born her mother was always singing to her. For hours her mother would rock her in her arms and sing to her. Whenever she played with her or fed her or bathed her she would sing to her.

All her mother's baby talk to her was lilting and songlike. They say that whenever her mother sang to her she used to smile and gurgle, in her own way joining in.

She also remembers that for many years every night

as she lay in bed she would make up songs for her mother and she would imagine them floating down the halls to her. As I have studied her and followed her career over the years, I have felt that all her singing is basically directed to her mother. Not surprisingly, her first record was dedicated to her. And as her mother was dying she held her hand and sang hymns to her.

Here I believe is a perfect example of the genesis of music in the performer and composer – and of the love of music that exists in all of us.

Our first appreciation of music comes through the sounds of the mother, especially her voice and her lullaby. Our earliest musical expression, of which speech is a part, is in a sense a duet with her. And later in life we should still be able to discern the voice of love in the music.

All music comes to us as a lullaby and we pass it on as another lullaby. It is given to us as an expression of love and we give it on as another expression of love. From the heart to the heart.

## KEVIN

Kevin is a fourteen-year-old boy who came to see me because he has many fears and obsessions. He is tormented with thoughts of death. He fears every night when he goes to sleep that he will not wake up in the morning. He also fears that if he touches many substances with his hands they will turn into poison and kill him. He is also very afraid that if he thinks of certain people his very thoughts may cause them to die. He leads a very anguished life.

It takes no more than a few days of psychiatric training to recognize that Kevin is a boy holding a great deal of anger, and that it is this anger which activates his fears. Until he is able to turn the anger into love, he will never overcome his fears. When I ask Kevin if he is angry, he says, "No, I never get angry," and his parents will agree with this. But when I test him in a certain way* I then

* "The Umbilicus Problem," THE COLLECTED PAPERS OF JOHN DIAMOND, M.D., VOLUME II.
Refer also to Appendix III in this collection.

find that he has a great deal of unconscious anger – that is, anger of which he truly is not aware but which nonetheless is operating inside him all the time, causing among other things his fears of death for himself and his loved ones.

I noticed that every time we talked about something which would certainly make him angry, he would rock his body or tap his foot or his hands. I realized that these rhythmic gestures are his way of trying to overcome his anger. Therefore I was not surprised to learn that his greatest joy in life is his drumming. He is a very skilled drummer and he truly loves playing. I was easily able to demonstrate to him that when he drums, even for only a few seconds, he loses his unconscious anger and is then able to be more loving to his family and to himself. He smiled and nodded as if to say, "I have really known that all along." It has been his music which has kept him alive and sane.

I wanted Kevin to learn what music can really do, so I tested his mother and found that her thymus was underactive.* I then asked him to play an exercise that his teacher had assigned to him. We found that while he played this his mother tested just as before. She had not been strengthened by his playing. Next I asked him to play something that he enjoyed playing – something he would like to play just for the sheer joy of playing it. Now his mother tested strong, her life energy had been activated. But when I conducted more sophisticated tests

---

* See Appendix II.

we found that there were still evidences of diminished life energy in her. His playing did not overcome the weakness. More was required.

So I said to him, "Kevin, don't concern yourself with the mechanics of what you are doing. While you are playing just think that all the sound is going to your mother, that you are directing it to her, because you really want it to raise her life energy and make her healthy." Now when he played she was greatly strengthened. He had learned how therapeutic music can be, and how important it is when one is playing to direct it outwards in a loving gesture to other people.*

Now there is beauty and peace in the household because every time Kevin plays he is thinking of healing his parents, and all the time that they are listening to him play they know it is a message of love from him to them. His fears have been replaced with love.

* Refer to "Transmitting the Pulse" and "How to Practice" in this collection.

## MUSIC AS THERAPY

An editorial in the Journal of the American Medical Association* raised my hopes that music may become accepted in its true role as therapy.

The author, Dr. Samuel Vaisrub, quotes the poet Novalis, "Every sickness is a musical problem, every cure a musical solution." He also quotes Francis Bacon, "The poets did well to conjoin music and medicine in Apollo, because the office of medicine is to tune this curious harp of man's body and to reduce it to harmony."+ He talks about healing ceremonies concerning the temples of Asklepios, and also (as all writers do) mentions David's harp playing to soothe Saul.

However, it is unfortunate that he writes of "stopping short of identifying therapy with music," and closes by reducing music to "an adjunct to psychotherapy in some

* (1980) Vol. 244, p. 1963.

+ ADVANCEMENT OF LEARNING.

mental institutions." What a pity that he is not aware of the tremendous therapeutic power which music has to activate the life energy in an individual and release the suppressed curative powers, the healing force of nature within us.

As an example of its power we have the findings on the longevity of classical conductors as reported in YOUR BODY DOESN'T LIE. At the age of seventy, by which age 50% of American men are dead, 80% of conductors are not only alive but active and working. There is something incredibly therapeutic in music. We have demonstrated that most music, as distinct from amusement* can have profound effects. It will be found that all energy imbalances are corrected by music. Music activates the life energy and the thymus gland, balances the hemispheres of the brain and reduces one's vulnerability to stress. It raises the pain threshhold and can be used as both analgesia and anesthesia. Acupuncture imbalances throughout the body are instantly corrected. Even more importantly, we have shown that the unconscious negative attitudes that impede our relationships with ourselves and with our loved ones and with the whole world throughout life are overcome by music. Music is unique in this function. Used correctly and appropriately reinforced, it is possible with music to achieve within minutes the results of perhaps years of psychotherapy.+

As I have pointed out elsewhere† there is within each of us an ongoing conflict almost from the moment of birth

---

* Ruskin called it *amusia* – "the denial, or desolation for want, of the Muses."
– FORS CLAVIGERA.

\+ THE RE-MOTHERING EXPERIENCE.

† THE COLLECTED PAPERS OF JOHN DIAMOND, VOLUME II.

to the moment of death between the forces for life and health and those of sickness and death, an ongoing battle between love and hate. Whenever the negative force is operant, sickness reigns. Thus it is that most of us become ill and eventually die through surrendering to the forces of death. This struggle within us can be won by music as the life forces are activated – hence, the cures that have been attributed to music over the millenia. It activates the power of love for ourselves and for our fellow men. It alone of all the art forms can do this with such immediacy and facility.

It does this whether the listener "likes" the music or not, whether he understands the music or not, whether it is part of his culture or not. This is its power. We can be cured by an Indian raga, by an Aboriginal didjeridu, or by the chant of a Dakota Indian, and of course, by our Bachs and Beethovens, and by our Schnabels and Furtwanglers. This is the splendor with which we have been endowed over the centuries. It is part of our divine healing heritage. It is ours whenever we desire it.

Music will not cure diabetes, but neither does insulin, although it may control the symptoms. What music can do that insulin cannot is raise the healing powers within, perhaps to the point that the involved organs may be repaired sufficiently to function on their own again. It raises the life energy and facilitates the forces of love, the forces of life within the individual to heal himself.

Great music is written by composers with great love and high life energy, from the heart. If it is performed by people of equally great heart and purity of intent, who surrender themselves to the spirit of the composers, it has incredible power. It is in the fullest sense of the word, therapeutic.

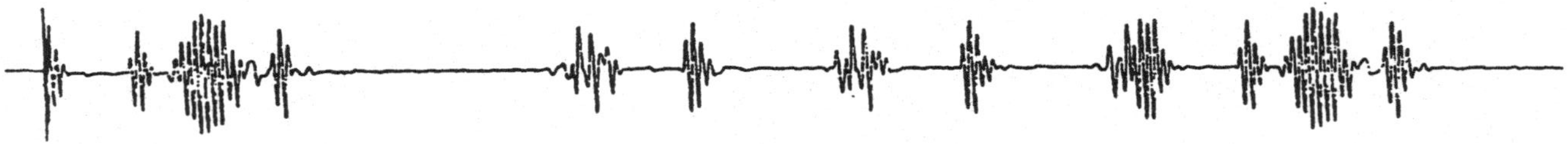

## AN EXAMPLE OF THE THERAPEUTIC POWER OF MUSIC

These are the tracings of the heart sounds of a man who had a coronary occlusion quite recently. The first shows a marked cardiac arrhythmia – note the triple beats. This arrhythmia had persisted for some weeks in spite of heavy medication. The second tracing shows the complete alleviation of the arrhythmia after several minutes of listening to appropriate therapeutic music.

## THE DIVINE TASK OF THE PERFORMER

*"The highest graces of music flow from the feelings of the heart."* — *Emmons*

A concert hall is a temple. It is here that the prayers of the great composers are given life by the ministrations of the priestly performer for the spiritual uplifting of the audience.

Great music is created not in the mind of the composer but in his heart. It transcends all questions of method and formulae and laws. It is a prayer to God meant also to be heard by the composer's fellow man. It is a public prayer. In it he acknowledges to God his own failings and his own troubles, and at the same time he tells us of them. Through prayer he resolves the inconsistencies and the disharmonies that exist between his understanding of himself as he is and his perception of his evolutionary goal. He is intensely aware of how far he has strayed from his true destiny. He has great insight into his own internal disharmonies and inner failings and more clearly than most he senses his true path. His composition is his prayer, an acknowledgment of his deficiencies and inadequacies and is an attempt through the internal workings of his soul and of his heart to draw closer to the true way, to draw closer to God.

At the same time, the composer puts out his heart to his fellow men. He asks us to see his suffering and his dilemma, and through the composition his attempts to resolve the inconsistencies within himself and to be purely one with God. And we are uplifted and healed by this experience because the composer's problem is not his alone but is one aspect of the universal problem, of the only problem – our alienation from God. We are each alienated in a slightly different way but the causes and the suffering and the resolution are much the same, if not identical. And it is through his public prayer, the public acknowledgment of his separation from God and through the public searching in his heart and the drawing closer to God, that he achieves the partial resolution of the distress. It may not be our way to solve the problem but if we allow ourselves to flow with his prayer we will come closer to finding God, as the composer has. This is the holy gift that the composer offers to us. Through his public prayer we may all be healed.

Thus as it is that all illness is an alienation from God, we may say that music is the great therapy. It belongs in a temple.

I am reminded of the healing temples of Asklepios. The afflicted went through a process of incubation in which they slept in the holy place, tended by priests and aided towards healing by poetry and music.

Our society unfortunately no longer associates music with healing, but it has retained its religious association. It is hard to imagine a church service without music, without the lifting up of the voice to God and, with this, the opening of the heart to receive the spirit, the Divine Healer.

Unlike the prayers of Jesus or St. Francis or Isaiah, music comes to life only when it is re-created by the performer. This is his holy function, to take the inert prayer of the composer and bring it to life so the populace may be reminded of God, may be drawn to God and healed. This is the priest-like, catalytic role of the performer. He must honor the prayer and be as true to it as a rabbi reading Ezekiel for us. He must recognize that the composer has a truer sense and feeling for God than most of us. And he must never allow his own idiosyncrasies and his own failings to intrude. The prayer is a cry from the heart of one man. If it is blurred or distorted, it will not sing to God as it was intended. The priest is not to be concerned with the trappings of his office, only with the purity of the message.

A great composition must be cherished as lovingly and as caringly as a relic of a saint, for that is what it is. The priest displays the relic. He does not alter it. He holds it up before himself for us to see, for all of us to be uplifted by its glory. Reaching up for God. In its own way it is sacred as is every pure prayer to God. This is the precious priest-like ministering role of the performer.

## THE TRUE ROLE OF THE RECORDING ENGINEER

Perhaps the greatest invention of our time is the recording process. We are able to enshrine time as never before possible. We can preserve the performance forever. How different would the world be today if the Sermon on the Mount had been recorded – if today, two thousand years later, we could respond to the very voice of Christ? Could there ever have been war? Could there ever have been anything but love and light on the earth? What other treatment would a doctor need to give than to have the patient sit in a quiet holy place and listen to the voice of Christ as he prayed to God?

Beethoven is not Christ, nor is Furtwangler. But they are two of the most holy figures in the recent history of Western music. We do not have recordings of Beethoven reading his own prayers, but, thank God, we have many enshrinements of Furtwangler, the greatest of the priests who ever read Beethoven's prayers for us. The healing of Beethoven comes through to us now and will, I hope, for all generations through that totally unselfish, totally dedicated servant of Beethoven, and of God. Thus our lives and our souls may always be enriched by Beethoven who struggled against his terrible internal problems and disharmonies to find God as best he could, in his own way. His prayers lie on the written page to be brought to life by the most dedicated of priests.

A recording engineer enshrined those performances for us. He took the sounds of Beethoven coming through Furtwangler and captured them so that they may exist forever; so that we would know not only Furtwangler, but Beethoven – and through him, God. This is the function of the dedicated and inspired recording engineer. He is part of the God-given, therapeutic chain passing from the composer through to the populace. Without him only a limited number will be uplifted, but through his efforts the number that may be healed is infinite because they may continue for generations. Thus he is indeed essential for the benefit of mankind. He is the priest's scribe. He works in the studio with the performer and as such the recording studio is the inner temple with just the priest and the deacon present.

This is the responsible role of the recording engineer. He is the deacon of the inner temple. And yet what do we find today? His inner chamber has no natural light, no natural air. It is filled with smoke. He sits, surrounded by cups of coffee, before an enormous console. He has power. He has control. How can he see himself as a humble servant of God working for his fellow man, as the necessary voice of reality to the performer? He does not see himself as the intimate audience, the immediate congregation in the mind of the performer when he invokes the prayer. His mind is filled with thoughts of the microphones and the levers he controls and the power that he feels rising up from the console in front of him. His lack of humility and dedication to the holiness of his role can distort the prayer and make it at best of limited value.

This need not and should not be. The role of the recording engineer, of the scribe, is in its own way just as important as that of the performer, of the priest singing the prayer. He is at this time the total congregation of the priest and he must in every way encourage the performer to sing out to him. It is so easy for a performer to lose thought of the audience in a recording studio and allow the sound to fall on the barren ground. He can lose his dedication. The recording engineer must become the immediate audience to whom the performer opens his heart. Then the music will take seed and grow, not only there but throughout the world and throughout time.

There is nothing passive about the role of the recording engineer. Like all true members of the congregation he must be active. He must aspire to receive the greatest from the performer. He must desire so fervently in his heart that the prayer of the composer will be given full and total life by the performer. He must do everything he can to assist the priest to enable the true prayer to be expressed. The more he can actively assist, the more he can reduce the stress and help to raise the life energy and creativity of the performer, the better will be the reading of the prayer. His is a very vital, active role. He is an essential link in the therapeutic chain. His work is not for the recording company, but for humanity.

## THE LEADER AND THE PULSE

I was recently working with an opera singer who had asked me to help her because, as she put it, "the internal stress I feel when I perform professionally is unbelievable." We began by working with her breath. I placed my hands on her lower ribs in order to feel their lateral expansion as her diaphragm contracted. There was an easy full rhythm, both sides of her rib cage moving equally and synchronously.

I asked her to sing "Happy Birthday" and the rhythm was maintained as she started to sing. Then I asked her to sing the last aria she had sung – and instantly her breath jammed! Her ribs suddenly stopped moving and when they resumed the rhythm was jagged and asynchronous. She was now under stress which was revealed in her altered breathing pattern. We repeated the experiment, this time with her only thinking of singing the aria and the findings were the same.

She told me that, in a way, she was already aware of this. She said, "Every time the conductor points at me to start, I feel my breath jam and then I am breathless and stressed the whole time I am singing." We then tested her breathing while thinking of singing the same aria – but under a different conductor. This time her breathing was not jammed! She exclaimed, "Yes, that's reasonable. With some conductors my breathing is easy." The reason for this, of course, is that some conductors are themselves unstressed and have the ability to transmit the pulse. But a stressed conductor is unable to transmit the pulse accurately. This causes the performers' breathing to be jammed. This is revealed in the Life Energy Breath Span Test.* On the other hand with a high energy conductor one can almost sense all the players breathing as one. This pulse is transmitted to the audience who also seem to breathe as one and thus we have conductor, orchestra and audience all breathing with the pulse of the composer – all in concert.

I once asked a world famous pianist to recall performing a certain concerto under Furtwangler. He tested strong. I then asked him to recall performing the same concerto under another very famous conductor and he tested weak. As you may have guessed, our testing has shown that the second conductor is of a lower energy level. The test revealed what had been locked in the soloist's unconscious for thirty years – that Furtwangler was a high energy conductor and the other was not.

It is essential that the conductor be unstressed during performance because if he is stressed he will interfere with the natural breathing of all the performers under

---

* refer to "The Life Energy of Music and Performance" in this collection.

him. This will prevent the free transmission of the pulse, the very soul and vitality of the music. But if he is unstressed then all those under him, even if they themselves are usually stressed by the act of performing, will rise above this in response to the pulse that he transmits to them, ensuring a high energy therapeutic performance.

## A TENNIS ANALOGY

I asked the tennis professional at my club why it was that both my son and I have so much better rallies when we are hitting with him than when we are hitting with each other. When we are each hitting with him, the rallies are much longer and somehow seem to be more flowing and more beautiful with many fewer erratic strokes. There seems to be some coordination which develops between the professional and each of us which we cannot develop between ourselves. When I watch him it is almost like watching a dance. The ball seems to flow back and forth across the net, this way, that way, to this corner, to that corner. The running of the players seems so even and easy. There is beauty and poetry. But when I do it with my son it is ugly and unsatisfying for both of us.

The pro told me that this is because he tries to set up a rhythm of play. He said, "You will notice that nearly all the strokes I make are of much the same speed and of about the same length. There is a regularity and a rhythm that I try to establish in the rally to achieve the very thing that you are pointing out."

It suddenly occurred to me that this is very much like

the role of the conductor. Neither my son nor myself is skilled enough to be able to impose our own strong rhythm. We recognize that the pro has this ability and so we put ourselves in his hands. We submit to his stronger rhythm and as long as we do submit, we will play better than we can on our own. A conductor once told me that he tries to have the player play beyond himself. And that is exactly what the tennis pro does. When I play with him, when I am under his rhythm,I play beyond my own limits.

But sometimes I find that when I play with the same pro the rallies are unsatisfying and I quickly feel tired and dispirited. Something is wrong. I have tried to blame many things for this, from my own physical capacities to the tennis balls to the lighting and so forth. I can tell something is wrong. There is no flow. There is no rhythm. I am not playing even to my own limits, let alone to the limits I can usually play with him. At last I have discovered the cause.

Yesterday was one of the terrible days. Afterwards he told me that he had spent most of the previous night drinking and he was exhausted. I thought back and realized that most of the sessions that had been unrhythmic and ugly had been when the pro's life energy had been low for one reason or another. I had submitted to his rhythm and his pulsation and thus when his life energy was low he brought my life energy down and destroyed whatever rhythm I myself had.

Thus it is we find that many high energy orchestral players tell me how tired and dispirited they feel after playing under certain conductors. We always find on test that these conductors are low-energy conductors. And of course the conductors under whom the orchestral players tell us that they have played beyond their limits test as high energy conductors. As was said of Vaughan Williams' conducting, "He draws out of you what you know isn't there."*

The tragedy is that most conductors are highly stressed and thus of low life energy. Over the years they erode the life energy and vitality of the players who have submitted to their pulsation. This is one reason why we find that most orchestral players seem to have lost all love of music. It has become just another job. They do not talk about their profession with love or enthusiasm – it is just work. And so nearly all of them will test weak when they think of playing music or, most tragically of all, when they even think of listening to music. The love and glory of music has gone. One of the major activities at the Institutes for the Enhancement of Life Energy and Creativity and the Archaeus Research Foundation is to re-kindle this love of music in the musician, to help him increase his own pulse and respiratory rhythm, to make him impervious to the low energy conductor and to enable him to soar to the greatest heights with the high energy conductor. Once his energy pulsation is re-activated, when he again loves music to the very core of his being as he did when he was a child, when music can enthuse him and open his heart as it once did, then he is a power of good in the world.

* R.V.W.: A BIOGRAPHY OF RALPH VAUGHAN WILLIAMS, by Ursula Vaughan Williams, London, 1964, p. 182.

## TRANSMITTING THE PULSE

It cannot be overemphasized that every performer must have as his basic intent the raising of the life energy of his listeners. This is my intent now as I am writing for you. My writing may not be technically correct, it may be full of "wrong notes," there may be passages which appear illogical, but I try as far as possible to have your life energy raised when you read what I write, or when you listen to what I say at my lectures and seminars. This must constantly be the goal and the aspiration of every writer, of every composer and of every performer; in fact, of everyone who communicates. And that includes all our communication, both formal and informal, with our loved ones and neighbors and the community at large.

As long as this is the aspiration of the performer he will be able to purely transmit the pulse. He will have little if any narcissistic concern with the technical criteria of performance. Instead of a situation of "Listen to how well I play. Aren't I brilliant?" it is rather "Listen to the glory of the message that I am honored to pass on to you." I have shown in the story of Kevin* that when he concentrates on his mother's energy being raised by his playing, it will happen. I have also pointed out that when a person wants his voice to be therapeutic, to raise the energy of the recipient, it will happen. It is essential to practice with an open and giving heart. And of course it is vital in actual performance. Cast out fears of making a mistake, cast out thoughts of how great you are. Think only of the privilege which you have been given and think only of giving the message of love from the composer to the audience. Desire nothing more than that they be uplifted by your ministering efforts.

Imagine an orchestra in which not only did the conductor have high life energy but all the performers as well. This has probably never occurred but it is completely feasible. Then we would really know the glory of music as we have never experienced it.

If you are a composer, do not be obsessed with any formal system, nor with whether this style will make money for you, or such concerns. Think only of a transmission of pure energizing love to the world. This is your duty.

And what of the audience? The more that you respond with love and gratitude to the performer and composer, the more that you will be able to receive. You

* see "Kevin" in this collection.

must tell them, "I do not care about anything else but the pure pulse. I want nothing else but to be uplifted. I do not want to be thrilled. I do not want to be superficially excited. I do not want sentimentality. I do not want prima donna performances and ego trips. I want the pure pulse of love." Then you will facilitate the true function of the performer – the transmission of love. Nothing else in music matters. Nothing else in life really matters.

## LIVING IN THE MOMENT

Tchaikovsky once made a statement to the effect that music is made up of important passages with padding between them. It may be because of this view and its implications that, on test, Tchaikovsky is not a very high energy composer.

Tchaikovsky's statement is helpful for us to understand one of the apparent differences between a high energy performer and one who is stressed and consequently not able to transmit fully the potential energy of the music. On listening to a stressed performer, one gets the impression that he moves from climax to climax and pays scant attention to the passages between – the "padding" of Tchaikovsky – which of course with a great composer is anything but padding and in fact is just as important, and in many ways more important, than the "big bangs." On the other hand, when one listens to a high energy performer the impression is soon gained that these apparently less important passages assume just as much importance as the more obvious ones.

There is the feeling of what we call "living in the

moment," a total dedication to, and relationship with, the particular note of music being played at each instant. There is no apparent drive to reach out for the next climax. There is complete respect for each word in the flow of the composer's prayer.

We find the same attitude when we test individuals performing simple tasks. Suppose I ask someone to walk in order to arrive _at_ a chair in the corner of the room. If I test him when he gets there he will test weak. He has been stressed by the effort. But if I ask him instead not to set his sights on arriving at the chair but rather to pay attention to each step, and each portion of each step along the way, he will be energized by the process.

It is the same with music. A surrender to living in the moment will produce a high energy performance, but striving from climax to climax will produce a highly stressed, low energy performance. The breath will not flow freely.

Paradoxically we find that paying attention to every particular aspect of each step also correlates highly with having a larger goal than just walking to the chair at the end of the room. We find this in the following way: if the person, before he starts to walk to the chair, says to himself, "It is not important that I walk to the chair. It is important that I arrive there with high energy," it will be found that he will do so. And it will be found that he will have paid attention to every step along the way.

We find the same when listening to a very high

energy performer such as Furtwangler. One gets the impression that he is not living from immediate goal to immediate goal, but rather that he has the overriding goal of transmitting the pulse of the composer* as purely as possible, of presenting the overall view as clearly as he can. His concern is with the totality, not the thrilling "bits" that we have come to expect. At the same time there will be the infinite attention to the detail of each moment. It is strange that these two seeming paradoxes go together – living in the moment, totally submitting oneself to the pulse at each moment, and the overall goal, the heart of the composer.

* As Beethoven said about his composition, "I always have the whole in my mind."

## GROUP DYNAMICS OF PERFORMANCE – TWO EXAMPLES

Every musical combination, from duet to full symphony orchestra, will have its energy level set by one member of the group who is the leader, whether appointed or not. It is his energy level that determines the transmission of the pulse by the group.

In an orchestra this level is invariably set by the conductor and thus we find that the same orchestra may test at many energy levels depending on that of the particular conductor.

But what of a small group? Let us consider for example a very fine piano trio which tests as having high energy. Other recordings by the violinist and the cellist do not have high energy. But those of the pianist do have high energy. Thus it is reasonable to assume that it is his high energy level which firstly raises the energy of the other two performers and thus enables them to purely transmit the pulse when under his leadership.

Now let us look at the Budapest String Quartet on record. They basically made three sets of recordings –

in the days of 78's, in the days of mono and a last set in stereo. The 78 and the stereo sets both are of high energy levels but the mono set is of low energy. Why should this be? The major change of personnel between the 78 set and the mono set was the substitution of Jac Gorodetzky for Alexander Schneider as second violinist. The stereo set, which is also of high energy, marks the return of Schneider to the group, replacing Gorodetzky. This finding is particularly unusual as here it is the low energy second violinist who set the energy level of the quartet, overriding that of the leader, the first violinist.

It is also interesting to note that more string quartets have high energy, *pro rata,* than any other chamber group.

## PERFORMANCE AND POISE *

There is so much research that we have done concerning the posture and poise of performers that it is not possible even to summarize it. Let me simply give an example.

I tested many performances of one of the world's great flute players. As is the case with almost all flute players, I found that he was stressing the listeners. The stress specifically affected their thyroid meridians. And of course I found that he was similarly stressed himself – and it was this specific meridian stress that he was transmitting to them.

There is a gesture which tends in most people to weaken the thyroid meridian. This is a tilting of the head to one side. It is a common attitude in people who are depressed, and depression is a negative attitude of the thyroid meridian.+

---

* For the correct usage of the words 'posture' and 'poise' see Dart, R.A. (1947), The Attainment of Poise, S. Afr. Med. Journal, 21:74-91.

+ See LIFE ENERGY: Understanding and Transforming Your Emotions to Achieve Total Health.

I observed that the flute player whose performance I was testing was tilting his head the entire time he was playing. So I suggested to him that he keep his head vertical and play the same passage again. Now, almost miraculously, not only was he not weakening the audience, he was positively strengthening them. Their life energies – and his – had been turned around by this simple postural correction.

Nearly all flute players tilt their heads. Perhaps this is the reason that so few of them test as having high life energy. It may also explain why most I have investigated have low thyroid activity.

There are fundamental problems relating to every instrument as each has its own particular negative stress potential relating to the playing position. Thus whenever we work with a performer to raise his life energy we must always work with his body usage.*

---

* THE UNIVERSAL CONSTANT IN LIVING, F. Matthias Alexander, New York, 1942.

## THOUGHTS WHILE PERFORMING

I have asked many professional musicians what they think about when they are performing. The answers are very surprising. Many of them are worrying about the difficult passage that is to come. They fear that dreaded curse, a wrong note.*

Many of them are thinking narcissistic thoughts – how lovely their music sounds (rather than how beautiful the music is). Some think personally about certain members of the audience. Vladimir de Pachmann used to talk to pretty girls in the audience while he was playing.

At times, many of them think thoughts which have nothing whatsoever to do with the music – what they will be doing tomorrow, or the vacation coming up, and the like. Their playing is purely mechanical.

I find that very few of them are actually totally immersed and at one with the music. There is a part of them which prevents them from totally committing themselves to the music. These will be the people who

* See "Rong Noats" in THE LIFE ENERGY IN MUSIC, VOLUME II.

test as Type 2 in the total commitment test.*

It is rare to find a total surrender to the glory of the music. These are the performers who are committed to the uplifting of the audience through the music. Such a musician sees himself as a humble servant of music, and sees as his role the communication of its message of love. This musician is free of the usual stresses of performance. He transmits the pulse of the music and we all are enriched by the experience.

* "The Total Commitment Test," COLLECTED PAPERS OF JOHN DIAMOND, VOLUME II.

## A MUSICIAN'S SELF-WORTH

Have you ever wondered why so many musicians do not like to listen to their own records?

Let us approach this problem through the example of a highly gifted flute maker whom I have the privilege of knowing. When I ask him to look at a piece of wood which he plans to make into a flute he tests strong. When I ask him to look at a finished flute that someone else has made he also tests strong. But when he looks at a flute that he has made – he tests weak! And this applies to any instrument that he has made. It seems as if he does not value his own products, even though others do and most highly.

I ask a musician to think of any record he has made and very frequently he will test weak – but not when he thinks of someone else's record. Many composers will test weak when they think of any of their own compositions, but not when they think of another composer's.

It seems that they do not value their own products.* They are not basically justifiably proud of what they do. They have a low opinion of their accomplishments. This is not true humility. It is a downgrading of their real worth.

I have tested many musicians who have made numerous recordings, and most have tested in this way – not all musicians, of course, but so many of them. This devaluation is not something which is overcome through critical or public acclaim. Furthermore it may persist throughout their professional careers to their detriment, and to the detriment of all those who hear their works or who play their instruments.

The reasons for this negativity are buried deep in our childhood experiences, in our earliest relationships with our own bodily products.+ It influences our relationships throughout life to all our products – our music, our instruments, our work.

This problem, although it has been working away unconsciously for perhaps many years, can be corrected through the use of a specific affirmation and natural supplements. When this has been done, the instrument maker will then test strong for looking at one of his own instruments. The composer will test strong when he thinks of one of his performances or one of his recordings. He now values what he does, so he will be less stressed in

* refer to "The Bodily Products Test," THE COLLECTED PAPERS OF JOHN DIAMOND, VOLUME II.

+ Ibid.

doing it and we will be more energized by the final product.

When stresses occur, such as in making recordings, or in making a particular new instrument, the old negative attitudes have a tendency to recur. The affirmation reinforced with the supplements will overcome the situation. Had Brahms done that, perhaps he would have valued his works enough not to have destroyed so many of them. Because of his low opinion of his own worth, we have all suffered a loss.

## THE FOUR BASIC QUESTIONS FOR MUSICIANS

Whenever a professional musician consults me, we commence with the following simple tests.

1) I ask him to look at his instrument whilst I test him. He will usually test weak. He will then look at me with surprise and amazement as he starts to realize how much he is really stressed by music.

2) I then ask him to say "I like music." Now he will usually be even more amazed when he also tests weak. And when I ask him to say "I don't like music anymore" he will test strong.

3) I then ask him to think of any performance that he has given or any record that he has made. Again he will usually test weak. He does not value his work.

4) Then I ask him to think of performing in public, especially to imagine being about to play the first piece of the recital. Often now he tests as having what we call an umbilicus problem* – public performance not only

* refer to Appendix III.

stresses him, it makes him unconsciously angry.

Of course, many musicians pass all these tests – but most do not. Most have been so stressed by their work they no longer love it. All the beautiful reasons that caused them first to take up their beloved instruments and practice for thousands and thousands of hours have gone. The love and the joy are dead. It is just another highly stressed occupation. This is not unique to music. It is unfortunately the fate of most professionals. But it is such a tragedy in music because an unstressed musician can do so much for the world.

Most musicians believe that they still love music. Part of the tragedy is that as the love fades in response to the increasing stress of a modern-day professional career they do not become aware of it. This is the advantage of testing. It shows what they really believe, not what they think they believe.

This negativity as a result of the stress and disenchantment and falling out of love with music and music-making can be overcome, but first it must be recognized.

## A VERY HIGH ENERGY RECORDING

The highest energy recording of the 25,000 recordings I have tested is one I made of a sixteen year old patient. She was not only mentally and physically retarded but had also been severely autistic since early childhood. Of the latter she had been cured by the devoted love and care of her older sister.

Katrin loved to play the harmonica. She would play it for hours a day – so much so that she had a chronic rash around her mouth from it. She did not hold it according to the instruction books – which she could not read anyway – but grasped it as if it were an oversize sandwich. She did not know where the notes were. Of course she could not read music. In fact she never played anything but her own spontaneous inventions.

Like most of her music, the recording I made of her playing was directed to her sister, Susie, whom she loved so dearly and to whom she was so grateful. She played with such vigor and passion and such obvious outpouring from the heart. She would dance as she played and would call out, "Do you like it, Susie?" Her songs were obviously songs of love and gratitude. Suddenly in the midst of very rhythmic and intense playing she would stop and make the most incredible vocalizations to Susie.

I have played this recording to many people over the years and nearly everyone is impressed with it: one can sense the magic and the healing that is in it. However some musicians look down their noses at it and look at me queerly for having played it. These are the ones who have forgotten what music is really about. But most listeners quietly nod their heads and remember that long ago this was how they wanted to play and they realize that, even now, deep inside they still do.

A conductor must have this infectious love of music in order to inspire the orchestra players. He must test strong when he says "I love music" and he must first rekindle this love in the players, who are so stressed and overworked and jaded and bored with playing the same work yet again. For example, recently I attended a rehearsal at which the conductor told the orchestra "If you can forego your ten-minute break now we will have time to rehearse this piece. Otherwise we will not. It't your decision." Instantly one of the players jumped to his feet, marched off the stage, announced "We have a contract, you know," and lit up a cigarette. Through his own love of music the conductor must overcome this dispirited attitude of the orchestra and uplift them. Then, like Katrin, they will play from their hearts.

## THE DUTY OF THE MUSIC TEACHER

You may well ask "If, as you have shown repeatedly in this book, music has such therapeutic powers and so greatly raises our life energy, why is it that some performers have so many problems? They have stagefright, their egos get involved and prevent them transmitting the pulse, they fall out of love with music and do not value their performances any more and they can even become unconsciously angry at the thought of performance. Why, if music is so therapeutic, does it have such a negative effect on the practitioners of this therapy?"

I believe two major factors are involved. Firstly, consider the following: If you test the performances of very young Suzuki-instructed children you will find that the music they play is transcendental. As much as any music on this earth it is bursting with life energy.* But when you test the playing of most of their teachers, you will find that it is highly stressed and of low life energy.

---

* Unfortunately I have not yet had the opportunity to test enough examples of older Suzuki children to be certain, but preliminary findings indicate that they become stressed in their early teens.

Every child starts with an exuberant open-hearted love of music. Gradually and tragically this is destroyed by the horrors of most musical training systems.

Then what has not been extinguished by that is destroyed by the stresses of this high-powered technological age of music – the need for constant performance, the competitiveness and the fighting for survival in the highly commercial world that music has become. It is indicative of the severe stress imposed on professional musicians that so many test with low life energy in spite of the incredible energy-enhancing powers of the music they play.

Unfortunately we cannot remove these ever-growing commercial stresses from music. But we can expect more enlightened teaching, where it is recognized that the most precious asset of the young musician is his burning love for music. This must never be dampened, but must always be fostered and encouraged. This must be the sacred duty of every teacher.

## AUDIENCE COUGHING

All of us, both audience and performers, have been distracted so many times by audience coughing. Nothing seems more to break the magic spell of the music in the concert hall than a sudden outburst. I have asked many people why they think this coughing at the concert occurs. Most believe what I have found, that in most cases there is something more involved than just a cold or sore throat.

I have also questioned many people who have coughed at a concert. Most of them express their surprise that they did. As one concert cougher put it, "But there was nothing wrong with my throat beforehand, I didn't have a cough or a cold, so why should I have coughed at the concert?"

I have learned to pick with reasonable certainty a listener who will cough. Frequently before the coughing begins he rustles the pages of his program or noisily changes posture or even talks. Then after awhile, often after a short period of stillness and quietness on his part, a cough will explode. These people seem to want to make noise.

There are, as we know, other noisy distractions besides coughing – most of which if we were charitable, we would call unthinking, selfish acts. But if we were a bit more probing in our investigation, we would say that there was some attempt to destroy the spell. I am thinking not only of the noisy posture changes but also of program rustling (I understand that Toscanini's NBC concert programs were printed on silk so that they would be silent). I am thinking also of the noise of the unwrapping of candy. I can remember at concerts women near me opening their purses and noisily rearranging them with all their contents strewn on their laps. They obviously did not want to hear the music and they did not seem to want anyone else to hear it. I am reminded of a tape recording made of an exquisite performance of the Mahler Fifth Symphony. Just at the most sublime moment in the Adagio someone stentorially blows his nose.

In many concert halls, such as Carnegie Hall, I also hear the ushers as they noisily open and close doors and move around. They have no interest in the music and it seems as if they want to destroy our interest.

You may think I am being overly critical when I say that I believe there is a destructive element in the coughing and the other noises, but isn't that what you really feel? Doesn't it really make you angry? Let me suggest a few other observations.

Have you ever noticed how when a cougher cannot stop, he will noisily get to his feet and race out of the concert hall in a way which is even more destructive than the coughing? Or the coughers who, once they have stopped coughing, will then noisily unwrap their cough drops? And furthermore, why is it that they have their cough drops handy? I have asked many of them and they tell me it is not because they had a cough before they came, but because they know that they tend to cough at concerts! This is a recurrent pattern. And what of those coughers who really do have a cause for their coughing? A considerate person who had a cough before the concert would almost certainly not attend, out of consideration for the audience and for the performer.

What I believe is the most convincing observation of all is one that I am sure you have also experienced: nearly all the coughing occurs during the quiet passages – when it can best be heard, when it will be most distracting.

At one concert, I was sitting beside a pianist. He had been noisily talking to me whenever he could, criticizing the performer who was also a pianist, and telling me how much better he would play the work up there on the stage if only he were given the chance. He developed a loud cough which surely distracted the performer as much as it distracted us. I believe this coughing came out of his envy of the performer and his wish to destroy the beauty of the performance. My pianist neighbor tried to destroy the performer's music by making the only sound the audience is allowed to make, coughing. His envious attitude was, "If I can't be up there playing, neither shall he."

This may be why I have never seen a performer cough on stage. I believe there are two factors involved. One is that they are playing and therefore are less envious than we who are in the audience, unable to play even if we could. The second reason is that they are active. We the audience are pinned to our seats, immobile, silent. We are in an enforced passive role just like in school. Do you remember the first day at school? Before that day we had been free to run around most of the day, active and full of life. Then suddenly we were compelled to sit in a chair and listen to the teacher. We became passive – but we resented it. Deep down, we all want to be active. Perhaps this is why many people prefer listening to records at home to going to a concert. At home they are free – free to move as they wish, to rock their bodies, perhaps as their mothers rocked them when they first heard her music. To move around, to dance if they wish, unconstrained.

But something else, perhaps of even deeper significance, is involved when someone makes a distracting noise at a concert. It is a way of interrupting his treatment. He is just as effectively, and just as definitely, if unconsciously, sabotaging his treatment as a patient who refuses to take his medicine. The cougher is saying "I don't want to be well." He is resisting the therapy of the composer and the performer. This is why the coughers that we have tested all have low life energy. They do not have the will to be well. Furthermore when we test them at the end of the concert, they still do not have it. They have not allowed the music to heal them. They have resisted its therapeutic power. Furthermore, they tend to sabotage not only their own therapy but also the therapy for the other members of the audience.

Of course there are "just coughs" but, as you can see, there is often much more involved with coughing than just a tickle in the throat.

## APPLAUSE?

No matter how therapeutic the performance has been, no matter how strong the transmission of the pulse from the performer has been, no matter how much the life energy of the members of the audience has been raised, there is one thing that will instantly annihilate it. That is applause. I have tested this frequently at concerts and it is always so. You can test it for yourself with a recording in which there is applause at the end: The subject will test strong at the end of the music but the applause will abolish it. Applause is not sweet. It is jagged and loud and harsh. It destroys the very soul of music.

I have found very little in my search of the literature on applause. It was initially restricted to stage events and opera and only much later was associated with musical performance, and of course it is today a Western secular custom.

Of course, not all people by any means who applaud do it deliberately to destroy the spell of the music. Most of us do it because we have been taught that it is a sign of thanks to the musician. We are unaware that at the same time as we are giving him thanks we are destroying the work he has done.

Certainly in many cases to regard applause as being nothing more than the audience expressing gratitude is naive. So much of it is a greedy demand for more – "More! More!" Some of it is the desire to participate, to make sound which has been denied them whilst they have had to be silent during the performance as if to say, "Now it is my turn." Sometimes it appears to be a shouting contest of "Bravos".

If I wish to thank my wife for a kindly act, I do not applaud her. I may quietly say "thank you." But I may also thank her not by speaking but with a smile and the feeling in my heart toward her, which she acknowledges.

Some musicians have found the following suggestion beneficial: Before commencing the performance, they tell the audience that they are trying to give them an experience which will uplift them, and that this will be hindered by applause. They say in effect, "You do not need to applaud me. If you wish to thank me, I would prefer that at the end of the piece we all sit in silence for a short time so that we may hear the very walls of the concert hall still vibrating with the sounds of the music. If we then leave quietly we can keep the pulse of the music in our hearts. In that way the true purpose of the music will stay with us much longer."

The musicians who have done this say that there is a magnificent and beautiful change in their own attitudes toward their playing and in the audience's response to them. And afterwards there is a quiet, hushed reverence. It becomes a holy experience.

# LISTENING WITH THE WHOLE BRAIN

*"Music will enable you to see past facts to the very essence of things in a way which science cannot do."* — *Vaughan Williams*

A very gifted electronics designer told me recently that he was quite mystified by the double blind experimental technique. He said, "You know, my colleagues and I have spent many years listening to sound. We are very good judges of the difference between the sounds of various pieces of equipment. We research and develop a new amplifier and when we play it in the laboratory it is quite obvious that it is better than the other models with which we compare it. Then a psychologist comes in and does a double blind experiment in which we do not know which amplifier we are listening to. And almost without exception, we are unable to differentiate between them. I cannot understand it. The difference is so obvious when we hear it under our own conditions. But under the double blind conditions we fail. What's going on? Are our ears tricking us? Is there really no difference between the equipment, or is there something wrong with the experimental double blind technique?"

In my opinion it is the latter which is the problem. So I replied, "You see, when you are listening in your usual way, you are listening with both cerebral hemispheres, as a total person. You are perceiving and responding to all the nuances of sound of which you may not be totally consciously aware." This is what Theodor Reik said was the role of the psychoanalyst – he listened not just to the words but to all the implications and the subtle gestures and the symbolism – not only to everything that was said, but everything that was unconsciously stated. This is what he called listening with the third ear, and what we might call listening with the whole brain.

This is the only way to listen. This is the way that we must listen to music – not being concerned with technique, or the acoustics of the hall, or the tone of the piano, all left-brain criteria – but listening with the whole brain to the life, the energy, the gesture, the very vitality, the very soul of the musical experience. That is listening with the whole brain. This of course is what every good sound technician does. He listens with all his being and he hears things which cannot be measured with a meter. It is a total experience. This is how this particular electronics designer has been able to come up with so many new designs and has been so innovative, because he uses his whole brain – in the creation of the new concepts and ideas, and in interpreting the results.

But as soon as the double blind experimenter comes in and gives him a piece of paper and says, "Write down which is better, A or B," he is suddenly under the stress of having to perform. He listens with just his left brain, just his mathematical calculating brain. As we say, he "drops a hemisphere," and now he is not going to respond to the totality of the listening experience as before. If the differences are subtle he will not hear them. The fault is not in his ears, but in the experimental design that forces him into a different mode of experience than before, a less productive, less total mode of listening. He has ceased to listen as a human being. He listens only as a meter.

Unfortunately, many of our music critics are like this. Their love of music has faded, they are not totally involved with the life of the music. They are just concerned with technique. And when there is only technique there is no soul.

# THE THERAPEUTIC VOICE

The purpose of speech, as of all communication, should be to raise the life energy of the listener so that he is benefitted by the communication. Unfortunately we find that this is frequently not the case.

I spend a considerable time lecturing on the therapeutic powers of the voice to people who use their voices as therapy – for example, psychiatrists, psychologists, counselors and so forth. I usually demonstrate the therapeutic power of the voice in the following manner:

I take a subject who has on testing low life energy, whose thymus is testing as underactive.* Then, to determine whether the therapist's voice will raise the life energy of the subject, I ask him to speak while I am testing the subject. If the subject now tests strong while listening to the person's voice, we say that it is therapeutic. It is important that he direct his voice at the subject. This we call the focusing effect.+ If he merely speaks without project-

* see Appendix II.

+ see "Transmitting the Pulse" in this collection.

ing his voice with the intent of reaching the test subject, it will not have a therapeutic effect.*

I ask the person to count as we are not concerned with the content of his speech but the level of life energy which is transmitted through the rhythm and pulsation of the voice.

It will usually be found in a typical group of professionals who use their voices as their therapeutic tools that about 90% will not be able to raise the life energy of the subject – their voices are non-therapeutic! The others who have therapeutic voices will always be found to have higher life energy themselves. They will generally test as having active thymus glands. They will usually be those who look brighter and somehow healthier. They will be the ones who are breathing more easily and have better posture. In fact, one of the simplest ways to improve the life energy transmission of someone whose voice does not have therapeutic power is to ask him to correct his posture – to uncross his legs and to sit more squarely and more erect. Usually this one simple maneuver, and the heightened intent behind it, will now cause the subject to test strong. Life energy has been transmitted.

All the factors that activate the thymus gland + will therefore improve the therapeutic quality of the voice; indicating that the higher the life energy of the speaker,

---

* see "How to Practice" in this collection.

+ YOUR BODY DOESN'T LIE, p. 191.

the more life energy he will induce in the listener. Of course the same is true for the musician and his audience.

It will also be found that those who are able to raise the life energy of the listener are those who have a strong desire to do so. Those who feel that they must put on a good performance for the sake of their images will always fail, the same as the musician who is playing for predominantly narcissistic reasons. It will also be found that a speaker whose voice is therapeutic will cease to be therapeutic and will transmit stress in his voice if, for example, he loses sight of his intent or slouches back in the chair, or weakens his life energy in any other fashion.

The converse also applies: A subject testing strong can be weakened by a speaker with particularly low energy – this is what we call "untherapeutic" communication.*

How does a person respond when his own voice is taped and played back to him? It will almost always be found that a person's own voice will strengthen him. In rare instances I have found that a patient's own voice actually weakens. These have been patients who have been seriously ill.

On many radio programs I have said to the announcer that it is important that the audience have their life energy raised by us now. If their energy is not raised, then we should not be talking to them. We are stressing them.

---

* see "The Levels of Therapeutic Communication" in this collection.

And, almost without exception, the announcer will suddenly sit up straight and stub out his cigarette. Frequently a whole new tone and level of energy will come into his voice. Some of them have told me even several years later that they still think of this every time they go on the air. They have become aware that it is important that their voices be therapeutic.

Returning to our test, what if instead of having the person just count we have him say something such as "I really want you to be healthier and stronger." Now it will be found that many more people will be able to raise the energy of the test subject. This is because the speaker's energy has been raised by his intent and by the message he is communicating, and so his words now have a positive effect on the listener. It is the same with music; playing a composition will be more beneficial than just playing scales.

If now, instead of speaking the sentence, we ask them to sing it then even more of them will test strong because song has more therapeutic power than speech.

Thus we can see why it is that most musicians, although they may not have high energy in their own voices or in their own expression, will still raise, to an extent, the life energy of the audience. This is because of the sound of the musical instruments themselves and because of the healing message of the composer transmitted through the music. This is why to test the life energy of the performer whilst performing we have to use a more subtle test such as the Life Energy Breath Span Test.*

But even so, when we work with a musician to raise the life energy of his communication, we must first get his voice to be therapeutic. Only then can his music be truly therapeutic.

* see "The Life Energy of Music and Performance" in this collection.

# ON READING

Most people have a minor but definite dyslexia. This will be revealed if you test them immediately after they have read a sentence or two to themselves. It is better to have them instead read random letters of the alphabet than words to avoid any associational effects. (Strangely it will be found that if the letters are scanned from right to left rather than as normal from left to right, the weakening effect will not occur.*)

Let us now take this testing a step further. Have the person who is testing weak reading the random letters to himself now read them aloud. In nearly every case the weakening effect will still be present. Next have him read the letters aloud but this time directing his speech to someone. He now will test strong.

This is the same phenomenon as we observed with Kevin [+] and as I have advised regarding practicing.[†] It

---

* see "Why the B'nai Brith Syndrome?", COLLECTED PAPERS OF JOHN DIAMOND, VOLUME II.

[+] see "Kevin" in this collection.

[†] see "How to Practice" in this collection.

is easier to do this when reading aloud but with a little practice it can be done when reading silently. In both cases the important point is to concentrate on directing what you read out to someone. When we speak, either to ourselves or to someone else, our energy will be raised if we direct it outward just the same as when we play music.

Upon more subtle testing it will be found that even subjects who do not have this minor dyslexia and who therefore test strong when they read to themselves will experience heightened energy if they direct the reading outward.

Many musicians have dyslexia when reading music. It will be found that if they hear the music internally when they are reading it, they will overcome this weakness, an example of the power of music.* As well, projecting it to someone will enhance the effect.

In the preface I suggested to you that you would derive more benefit from this book (and for that matter from any book) if you read it aloud. Reading aloud makes one more aware of the music and rhythm of what he is reading. Preferably read aloud with a listener in mind. Then you will derive the greatest benefit from whatever you read.

---

* Incidentally most dyslexics will benefit by listening to music whilst reading.

## HOW TO PRACTICE

I have read many books on practicing and have talked to a great number of musicians about it. Somehow they all seem to miss the most vital aspect.

Let me explain. First, suppose we test someone from the audience and find that his life energy is low. Now suppose that we have a musician with high energy play some music for the audience. It will be found that the subject who was testing weak is now testing strong – his life energy has been raised by the performer. This is what we would normally expect.

Suppose I now say to the musician, "This time, do not think of playing to the audience. Play the same piece as if you were at home practicing." Then it will be found that the subject does not test strong. This is because the performer is no longer "putting out" to the audience. He is thinking only of getting the notes right. He is captive of his left brain analysis of his mechanics and he is no longer putting out from the heart. He has lost his intent and no life energy flows to the audience.

This is what is missing in practicing. I have gone to the homes of many musicians and have recorded them playing the same piece whilst practicing and then with an audience in mind. The difference in the life energy in their playing is remarkable.

The solution is very simple – to make practice a time when the musician plays to an imaginary audience, thinking of someone whom he would like to be benefitted by the music. He keeps his audience in mind the entire time he is playing. He may instead imagine that he is playing to the whole world, that his sound is going out from his practice room into the universe; or he may wish to direct it to a plant in the room or to his wife upstairs, or to the trees outside, or to God. It does not matter to whom it is directed. What matters is the wish to have the music go out, to give it to others. Then it is not a drudgery. It is from the heart and it becomes true music.

## MUSIC AND SPORTS

There are so many ways in which music can be used to improve sporting ability and enjoyment. Here is one example.

All sport can impose a stress which reduces one's ability because it interferes with the symmetry and balance between the two hemispheres of the brain, usually leading to the left hemisphere being dominant. Under this stress there will be less ability to perform as well mentally and physically than when the hemispheres are balanced. One of the simplest ways to achieve this balance is just to quietly sing or hum a tune to yourself as you are playing. You may choose any tune you wish.

At the moment of contact, for example when the racquet hits the ball, the player must not hold his breath. If he does, not only will his breath be jammed but the stroke will also be jammed. Also, if he is tested immediately afterwards it will be found that he has lost life energy because of this jamming of the breath. This is the usual finding. But if you quietly sing or hum a tune you will subtly alter the rhythm to fit in with your strokes so that the ball is hit at the moment of complete expiration which is the most advantageous timing for nearly all sports.

Through this simple maneuver your sporting ability will be improved. Many golfers have been able to take four and five strokes off their handicaps very quickly with such a technique. You will also find that not only are you playing better, but you are less stressed and you enjoy it more.

This is just another example of the widespread, almost limitless, uses of music. What it can do for sports it can do for all activities.

# MUSIC AND DANCE

A very experienced ballet dancer told me that he could not dance to Beethoven. He put on a record of the slow movement of the Ninth Symphony and shook his head and said "Every time I try to dance to it I jam up. There is no flow. It just doesn't work."

I went out and bought a record of a different performance of the work, one by Furtwangler. I put it on. He started to dance and his face beamed. He exclaimed "I can dance to it!" And he then improvised a dance for the entire slow movement – the most beautiful expression of visual poetry I have ever seen.

What was the difference? The first conductor did not transmit the pulse whereas Furtwangler, of course, does. When the pulse is not transmitted, as we know from the Life Energy Breath Span Test* there will be an interference with the breath, what we call a jamming of the breath. A sensitive dancer will feel this and it

---

* Refer to "The Life Energy of Music and Performance" in this collection.

will greatly inhibit his artistic expression.

It is critical that anyone who uses music as part of any activity be aware of the necessity of the pulse. Without the pulse the breath will be jammed. When the pulse is present, the breath will be free and likewise the expression.

## WOMEN, MUSIC AND TIME

According to popular tradition, women have a different sense of time.

What I have learned from my study of female conductors has led me to this same conclusion. There really is a difference between the male way of looking at events over time and the female way. These events can be a piece of music, an incident in the day, or the total life.

In a way this was best expressed by the most transcendental of all male conductors, Wilhelm Furtwangler, when he tried to describe the difference between Bach and Beethoven.* I hope I am not distorting his thoughts too much if I express them as follows: Both Beethoven and Bach present very powerful high energy and loving statements of man's evolution. But they present it from different perspectives. Bach shows us the ongoing evolutionary process. We see the spreading plain of human history, stretching from the horizon behind us to the

* CONCERNING MUSIC, London, 1953.

horizon before us. And we see ourselves as a speck in that panorama.

Beethoven presents not the ongoing, steady process of evolution, but instead highlights the moment of dramatic change, such as the first step that the first sea creature made when it crawled onto the land. It is Michelangelo's moment when God's and Man's fingertips are almost touching, the moment of exquisite passion – with man not a speck on the horizon but almost one with God. With Bach we would have seen not the tension and drama of this moment, but rather man being comforted in the arms of God. Instead, with Beethoven, we would have seen, as with Michelangelo, man's evolution at the very moment of its climax. We do not see the vast plains of the panorama of history, because the horizons are obscured by the mountains and chasms. When we struggle upward to the top, then we see the plains again. Both are necessary and, within themselves, complete statements. They are just different points of view. It is as if Bach is espousing the steady state origin of the universe and Beethoven the big bang theory.

Bach may in a sense be considered a more feminine composer, taking a longer, calmer view of time. He is not concerned with the more masculine aspects that excite Beethoven, the tension and resolution, achieving a climax and then pushing and thrusting forward to another climax, to another mountain, then another descent, and then on to another mountain and another climax. Bach instead takes the steady view, seeing life as evolving with its own rhythms, with its own pulse. He does not force evolution but rather flows with it.

We could say that Bach is an obedient loyal servant of Mother Nature. Beethoven on the other hand is the impatient assistant, with no time to quietly sit and tend the plants and wait for their growth. He pushes the soil and prods it, always striving for the dramatic moment when the first shoot appears.

In psychotherapy, we would say that Bach is a non-directive psychotherapist, respecting the convoluted, rambling and apparently undirected ramifications of the patient's mind. He understands what is called psychotherapeutic process, that it takes time for the patient to really see his problems. Then it takes time for him to understand what the therapist is trying to communicate, and then it takes time, sometimes a long time, for him to re-integrate and be cured.

Beethoven will have none of this. He is the impatient active psychotherapist. Within minutes he tells the patient what is wrong. And his genius is that he knows exactly what is wrong. And his further genius is that he can put it in exactly the way that the patient can use it and integrate it. But his sessions are not of peaceful calm steady progress. They are instead a time of tears and drama and shouting as well as of exquisite love and tenderness. He has no time to let things slowly develop and evolve. He says "I can see what is wrong with you and I am telling you now – and I am telling you how to fix it." He puts it in a way that goes straight into the heart of the patient. And if he is willing, he can change, and change immediately. Bach's sessions are safer, surer and less traumatic, and take time. Beethoven's sessions are short and to the point, with times of upheaval and internal chaos before there is resolution. It is a completely different approach, that of a completely different person. It is a completely different way of looking at time, and looking at the evolutionary process of a person, and a different way of looking at time and music and the evolutionary process of the music.

Man seems to go through life from battle to battle, from climax to climax. There is always tension and resolution. He is rather like a pinball, bouncing from spring to spring, concerned with the moment of tension and release from the spring, rarely seeing the total world in which he is moving. But this way is not the woman's way. She sees life more as a state of smooth flow, as a river gently running downstream. There are some rocks and some cascades, but never threatening powerful narrows and waterfalls. It is a different way, a more peaceful way, with greater respect for the process of evolution.

The woman is much more like Bach. She has a different sense of time. Time to her is not getting to the appointment. Time to her does not involve work schedules. Time for the true mother is not feeding the baby by the clock but when the baby needs it and when the mother feels that the baby needs it. She is more "right-brained."* She is more concerned with rhythm and gesture and pulsation than with the horological time of the left brain.

She looks at a baby and she sees the baby growing

* SPEECH, LANGUAGE AND THE POWER OF THE BREATH.

and maturing over the span of its life. The father may see him in the future as being a musician or doctor, but he does not see him growing into that position. He sees the mountain now and the mountain then, but he does not see the vast plain of evolution between. A woman looks at her baby and sees the whole panorama, the vista of his future experience, laid out before him. She is the Mother. She feels and she knows. The silly little conformances with the clock do not concern her. She is in tune with the pulsation of life.

## MUSIC AND MOTHERING

*The Mother of Songs, the mother of our whole seed.**

Throughout the ages music has been associated with mothering. The first sounds the baby hears are those of his mother – her breathing, her pulse and of course her voice transmitted to him through his watery environment. He is in a sea of pulsation, all generated by the mother.

And in the outer world when he is on her belly and at her breast, he still hears her pulsations, and especially her voice. There is no sound more loving, more comforting, more divine, than the sound of the special voice that the mother uses for her baby. It is pure love, "the eternal musical instrument of heaven and earth."+ And out of it arises the basic and greatest of all songs, the lullaby. The whole essence of music, no matter how complex and

* from a song of the Kagaba Indians, Colombia.

+ JOANNA'S CARE, John Ruskin.

sophisticated it may have become, is based on the sounds of the mother. And all the healing powers of music relate to the divinity of her love for her baby, and the wish to fully communicate this to him, to relieve every stress and discomfort and bathe him totally in the glory of mother love. He is held and cradled and rocked and nursed and bathed to the sound of the mother's divine peaceful harmony.

Thus you may not be surprised to learn that we have found that the music of female conductors tends to have greater comforting and therapeutic powers than that of most male conductors. Music is part of the mother's world. It is the great therapy.

Music invokes the divine love of the mother. It is her breath, her pulse, her spirit.

## FEMALE CONDUCTORS

It is my contention that the genesis of music is in the mother's communication with her baby. All music is derived from this relationship. Thus it is perhaps not surprising to find an incredible disparity between the energy levels of male and female conductors.

All female conductors I have tested – now over twenty of them – have high life energy whereas only a small percentage of male conductors have.

It seems obvious that it is much easier for a woman to be a high energy conductor. This I believe is a biological reality. It is somehow easier for the female to submit to and transmit the pulse, perhaps because it is more in keeping with her psychophysiology.

Most female conductors do not like to hear me say this. They want to be regarded as equals with the males. They believe that there is no sex difference in conducting. My results show that there is not only a difference but that the bias is heavily in favor of the females, even though they have been given such few opportunities in the male-dominated world of conducting. It is a tragedy to find such high energy female conductors being forced to conduct mediocre orchestras – and even at times having to form their own orchestras because of lack of support. And for them to then be criticized because the orchestral playing is not of a high calibre is really adding insult to injury. I sympathize strongly with their frustration* and disappointment, being unable to express the deep love of music which pulses so strongly within them. Of course there is a possibility that they may lose some of their high energy should they become conductors of major orchestras and become prey to the overwhelming stresses of the highly competitive professional life. There is no evidence of this to date but it is too early to draw conclusions.

What of female instrumentalists? Here the difference does not apply. I am unable to explain this adequately and any reason I gave at this stage of investigation would be simply a guess.

And what of female composers? Yes, we find that they also tend to be of high energy, confirming our theory that the genesis of music is in the feminine aspect of nature.

Again, it is a tragedy that we do not have a rich heritage of important compositions written by women over the centuries. There are many reasons for this. Some are social. And perhaps there are other reasons: It may be that women have not until very recently chosen this mode of resolving their problems – perhaps they have preferred

---

* and with the high energy male conductors languishing in suburban orchestras because they do not have "super-star" qualities.

other modes. Perhaps child-rearing and mothering itself accomplishes this goal, reducing or even eliminating the need to compose.

As I have pointed out elsewhere* Bach, and Baroque music in general for that matter, is much more feminine in its approach to life as revealed in music. I therefore believe that female conductors may render interpretations of Bach that would be extremely difficult for males to emulate. I recommend that they turn to the great master until such time as we have an equally great mistress.

I am not implying, of course, that the only music to listen to is that written by women or that performed by women. There are qualities in a transcendental male performer such as Furtwangler that seem to be even greater than those of any of the transcendental female conductors. One of the most important tasks when working with male performers to raise the energy of their performance is to help them bring forth and accept the more feminine aspects of their nature. When this is combined with their male qualities, their energies reach the limits of our testing to date. Further, there are other criteria equally as valid, equally as physiological, which are as yet beyond the limits of our testing.

Although the results reported here are some of the fruits of twenty-five years of research, they barely touch the surface. There is so much in music we will never fully understand it all.

---

* refer to "Women, Music and Time" in this collection.

## SPARE THE ROD

I saw a television interview with the first flautist of a major symphony orchestra in which he had played under the same conductor for more than thirty years. He said that even now, even after all these years, whenever he was going to play a solo passage, he would still become very nervous and fearful that he would make a mistake. During the performance which followed the interview, the television camera dwelt on him just before his solo was to commence. His nervousness was obvious.

Most orchestral players I interview tell me of the stress under which they play and the basic fear that they have of the conductor. In this regard, the stories of the outbursts of anger of many famous conductors and the fear, as well as the reverence, which the orchestra felt towards them is well known and requires no repeating on my part.

Music is supposed to be the communication of love. But how can a conductor inspire love when the players are fearful of him? There can be no worship of music and rejoicing in its message of love. I remember one youth orchestra rehearsal which I observed. One of the trumpet players kept coming in late on his entry. Every time he did, the conductor shouted at him and criticized him. And his problem only grew worse. He was so stressed that as soon as the conductor pointed the baton at him, instead of responding with his music, he would respond with fear and take in a quick breath. His breathing would then be jammed and he would come in late. And so it went on until the poor boy was utterly humiliated and on the verge of tears.

Perhaps the symbol for this problem is the conductor's baton. It is often used as a rod to command obedience through fear and awe on the part of the orchestral players. It is a tragedy that so many of the modern promotional pictures of conductors show them with stern threatening faces pointing the stick at a poor innocent musician, creating the image of a warlike general. All that is missing is his charger! There is no respect for the player, no understanding that he is trying to do his best. Instead the image is "You will do it my way, I am the boss. All power is mine."

There should be no power struggle between members of the orchestra and the conductor, no more than between the teacher and his pupils. Fear does not produce a creative, bright student who loves his work and his teacher and for whom he will give of his best. It instead guarantees a frightened student who does his work out of fear and without love. I believe this is a major contributing factor to the phenomenon that most orchestral players will test weak when they think of playing music. Their love of music has been destroyed.

How do we solve this? The conductor must throw away the baton. He must give a gesture not of power and autonomy but of open-handed love. He is not a feudal lord commanding his troops in battle and wielding absolute dominance over them. A conductor's role is not a military one, although I have heard of conductors describing their work in such terms. It is more a comforting and supporting and nurturing role* bringing out the best in every performer.

I once interviewed a conductor to learn her secret – she seemed to have an extraordinary ability to inspire her musicians to play beyond themselves, to so fully transmit the pulse. I asked, "What is it that you are doing other than what you appear to be doing when conducting?" She smiled a knowing, inward smile, looked at me and said, "Well, I am an Orientalist, you know." I replied, "I do not understand what you are trying to tell me." She became quite sheepish. She put her hands up to her thymus region and said very quietly, "It's like . . . I give to them from the heart." And then she lowered her head and was silent. No wonder she is such a high energy conductor. The message of her orchestra is one of pure love. There may be many orchestras which have better technique and better sound, but there are none which play with more love, with that " 'inner fire,' that enthusiasm and devotion which are of more value than any amount of technique."+

The conductor must be the priest leading the choir in a song of love. He must throw away the rod and spare the orchestra.

* THE RE-MOTHERING EXPERIENCE.

+ R.V.W.: A BIOGRAPHY OF RALPH VAUGHAN WILLIAMS, p. 164.

## STAGEFRIGHT

Many performers suffer from stagefright to some degree or other and many have certain rituals which they are compelled to perform before they can go on stage.

Superstitions and rituals are neurotic attempts to reduce the anxiety over the performance and are indications that the performer is highly stressed.

In every case we have found that the more the performer dedicates himself to the music and to the uplifting of the audience and at the same time the less he is concerned with himself, the less stress and anxiety he will experience before the performance. In fact it may completely vanish.

The more he is centered, the more he feels within his very being that his intent is to purely transmit the message of the composer to the audience, with no narcissistic concerns for himself, the higher will be his life energy and the more he will be able to be one with the music and to purely transmit the pulse.

## HOW TO CHOOSE A RECORDING

The Schwann Record and Tape Guides list a total of 42 performances of the Beethoven Ninth Symphony and 36 performances of the Dvorak Ninth. How will you decide which performance to hear? Each will probably have received rave reviews from various critics. Do you choose the one with the biggest name, the one on the biggest label?

You can derive enjoyment and musical knowledge from every performance, but only from the high energy performances will you receive the greatest benefit. By implementing the Life Energy Breath Span Test,* you can choose the ones with the highest energy. For example, of the 42 performances of the Beethoven Ninth Symphony, only 9 will test as high energy using the LEBST – that is, only 9 performances pass even this unsophisticated test. Of the 35 performances of the Dvorak Ninth, only 6 pass this test. Unlike the reviews of critics or promotional material, the LEB T offers an objective physiological

* refer to "The Life Energy of Music and Performance" in this collection.

means of selection. It is the only criterion related to that which is most basic in music – its healing powers.

My own record collection is divided into two groups – high energy performances and other performances. The other performances are extremely valuable as historical documents for research and teaching purposes. Many are exciting and pleasurable. But this is hardly the point – we have been conditioned to seek that which yields evanescent pleasures rather than health.

I no longer wish to listen for prolonged periods to performances which interfere with the full flow of energy through my body as a result of the performer jamming my breath. There are of course many therapeutic effects to be obtained from listening to any performance and this criterion is not the only determinant of a musical selection, but to me it is very important. On the other hand when I choose a high energy performance I know that in every way I will have gained from the listening experience. I will have been enriched in every sense of the word.

## THE DIDJERIDU

For years I have encouraged my patients and students to play musical instruments. I believe that it is essential for their ultimate health to be able to express themselves musically. Inside each of us is the deep desire to open our hearts and sing out with love. I find that when they allow music-making to enter into their lives, there is a beautiful change. There is an opening of the heart.

A wide variety of instruments have been taken up. Wind instruments have proven to be the most therapeutically valuable because the breath is personal, immediate and an integral part of the sound itself. This enables the patient to become very personally involved with the actual sound, which is my goal for him.

But as soon as he decides to play an instrument, the left brain takes over, defeating part of the purpose. If he goes to a teacher he is given rote instruction. He is told exactly how long the note must be held as the teacher taps his foot to give him not the pulse but the beat. He learns dexterity exercises which have no pulse or life in them. He is told that a note is "wrong" and that he must try harder. The instrument ceases to be therapeutic for him. Instead it becomes, as it is for the teacher, another piece of work, another left-brain task in our left-brain world. So I always suggest that, at least initially, the student get acquainted with the instrument on his own, guided by a simple instruction book.

But people are so conditioned that music must be "right" that they become frightened at the thought of doing it on their own. They ask, "But how will I know if my fingering is right? How do I know if my intonation is correct?" and numerous similar questions. At this point I often wish I had never suggested that they take up music in the first place. I can see it is just going to be another stress for them. They are captives of their left brains.

## *THE SOLUTION*

At last I have found the ideal instrument to recommend to them. It is the didjeridu of the Australian aborigines. This is a hollow, somewhat conically-shaped section of the trunk of a small tree. It is about three to four feet long and about two inches in diameter. It has no keys or finger holes. It produces two long carrying tones, supplemented by the use of vowel sounds and tonguing.

A very satisfactory substitute for the wooden didjeridu can be made from plastic tubing.*

A mouthpiece is fashioned out of some beeswax or epoxy putty and into this one buzzes his lips. From this description it may appear very primitive. In a sense it is, and in a sense it is very limited in its range. But when one listens to recordings of the Australian aborigines or of Stuart Dempster, the great American trombone virtuoso and didjeridu afficionado, one realizes the enormous range of expression of which it is capable.

Why is this instrument so beneficial? Primarily because there is no "right" and "wrong" with it. There are no notes as such, no fingerings, no written music. Within a very few minutes anyone can be playing it, but of course not as well as the aborigines or Stuart Dempster. Within a short period of time, anyone can be expressing himself musically with his breath from his soul. There is no teacher beating time with a stick. There is no metronome ticking in his ear, no music to read, no wondering, "Am I right or wrong?" There is pure release – and pure enjoyment. It is a whole brain activity.

After awhile, I teach the student a technique known as circular breathing. And here I quote Professor Trevor Jones, recognized authority on the didjeridu.+ Circular breathing enables "an uninterrupted sound to be main-

* "The Didjeridu," cassette tape by Stuart Dempster and John Diamond, Valley Cottage, 1981.

+ "The Art of the Didjeridu," Trevor A. Jones, Wattle Ethnic Series, Record No. 2.

tained for long periods of time. The technique is similar to that used by glassblowers, in that frequent short breaths are snatched through the nose while the cheeks hold sufficient air in them to expel enough down the tube to keep the note sounding as a breath is snatched. The continuous note produced in this way varies so minutely in quality during breathing that it is impossible to tell by ear alone just when the player breathes, so efficient is his control over the precise amount of wind pressure necessary to keep the air in the tube vibrating." This may sound complicated but it can be taught to most people very easily. Then a whole new world of playing opens up which is not possible with any other instrument, although circular breathing is used by some brass players. The breath is now free. He can play continuously for as long as he likes, easily for half an hour.

I have found that each time the patterns which emerge in the playing are original and unique. They may persist for a minute or so, or even perhaps for five or ten minutes, and then seldom if ever recur. There seem to be rhythmic patterns in the brain which require this external expression, and when they are expressed there is a sense of relief and relaxation.

This phenomenon rarely occurs in other types of musical expression, because we are forced to play the notes of the composer rather than the rhythms inside our brains. It also does not occur with most instruments because of the general gestalt of their use. The one other place in which it does occur is in the free music-making of young children. Listen to a child as he sings while he is at play. You hear beautiful little sound patterns, a soaring of the spirit, with no concern with right or wrong, correct pitch or manual technique. There is just pure enjoyment. This anyone can experience with the didjeridu within a few minutes and this above all is why it is so special. As Professor Jones said, "the didjeridu is a triumph of mind over matter depending for its effect entirely on the innate musical imagination . . . and not on handicraft or 'technology.' "

There is another aspect of playing the didjeridu which is extremely therapeutic. The life energy flows through the acupuncture meridian system. All the acupuncture meridians are represented on the lips.* Thus all instrument-playing in which the lips actively move will to some extent activate the entire meridian system of the body. This complete activation does not occur with the flute, in which the lower lip is fairly immobile. It occurs to quite an extent with brass instruments, but most fully with the didjeridu because of the active vibration of the lips. And thus it is that within a short time of playing the didjeridu, particularly when the breathing is natural and unforced as it is with the didjeridu, there is a tremendous upsurge of life energy throughout the body.

I have also recommended to all my students who are musicians that they take up the didjeridu. In addition to the reasons mentioned above, there are two other reasons why I suggest this to them. The most important is that playing the didjeridu is fun. They do not regard it

---

* refer to CHART # 2, from the Institutes for the Enhancement of Life Energy and Creativity.

as another piece of work. They can play it for the sheer enjoyment.

Secondly, I have found that those who are not wind players have more difficulty playing it than the average "non-musician" and it may require a certain degree of patience and persistence. The reason for this seems to be that such a student is usually very "unmusical" with his breath and his mouth. It is as if the music-making ability of a pianist or a cellist or a violinist is concentrated in his fingers and he does not know how to express himself through his breath. When he eventually does, there is a sense of release. He finds that now he plays better, there is more of himself in his playing, and he enjoys his music more. And the more he enjoys it, and the more he can express himself, the more completely he can give himself to the music, the better for us all.

## SOUND AND THE ACUPUNCTURE SYSTEM

One of our most interesting findings concerning sound and the body is that there appear to be two entirely separate systems through which the body receives sound. Obviously one is the ears. The other is the acupuncture system.

There are hundreds of acupuncture points on the body and many of them, especially those which are called the first tonification points for each meridian,* seem also to be sound receptors, at least up to about 1,000 Hz. Why this second system should exist I am not at all sure. The acupuncture system is intimately connected with the autonomic nervous system[+] and thus it may be that the sounds picked up by the acupuncture system enable us to be more closely attuned to the environment, enabling our basic physiological processes to subtly adapt.

This dual system can be easily demonstrated, for example upon playing rock music. As I have previously demonstrated, it will be found that a subject will test weak if he listens to certain rock music.[†] Suppose now

---

* refer to BEHAVIORAL KINESIOLOGY CHART #1 from the I.E.L.E.C.

+ BEHAVIORAL KINESIOLOGY AND THE AUTONOMIC NERVOUS SYSTEM, John Diamond, M.D., Valley Cottage, 1978.

† YOUR BODY DOESN'T LIE, p. 159.

that his hearing is blocked with suitable headphones. It will still be found that the rock music will have a negative effect, even though the subject reports he cannot hear it at all. If, in addition, sound-absorbing padding is applied over the first tonification point for the particular meridian that is basically assaulted by the rock music, it will be found that the subject tests strong. The rock music is no longer having an effect. Now if the sound-absorbing material is kept on the tonification point but the earphones removed, the subject will test weak again. There is a double sound reception system – the ears and the acupuncture system.

I first had an inkling of this many years ago when I found that the fewer clothes one wore when listening to music, the more energy one seemed to receive. In a concert hall where we are usually heavily clothed and closely seated, the acupuncture system is less able to pick up the music and the results are less beneficial.

Now what of noise? I have previously stated* that the difference between music and noise is that unlike music, when noise reaches a certain level (about 85 db) there will be a weakening effect evidenced by testing. With music there is no point at which increasing volume produces a weakness. These findings must now be modified to reflect more recent research evidence indicating that there are subtler acupuncture meridian weakening effects which occur even at quite lower volume levels. With these the deltoid muscle will not test weak "in the clear,"+ but on testing the individual meridians it will be found that a

* Ibid., p. 166.
+ Appendix I.

specific meridian has been weakened. The effect is milder – but definite.

Interestingly most noise, although by no means all, seems to affect the stomach meridian. This applies for example to the hum of most electric motors, the whine of car tires, the sounds of lawnmowers and so forth. These effects occur even at low levels and will involve both systems of sound pickup. Thus, if the ears are occluded the negative effect on the stomach meridian of listening to, let us say, a refrigerator motor will be present but will be abolished if, at the same time the ears are occluded, sound-absorbing pads are also placed over the main receptor points (S41) for the stomach meridian. These are situated on the dorsa of the feet. As a practical measure to reduce one's susceptibility to noise I have found that sewing or glueing sound-absorbing fleece in the tongue of one's shoes will have a beneficial effect as it reduces the absorption through these stomach tonification points.

It will also be found that specific nutritional support will activate the stomach meridian and reduce the susceptibility to most noise.

There are two important conclusions which follow from this research, both of which open the doors to many lines of further investigation. These are firstly, that noise even at very low levels has an effect on us – there may be in fact no minimum level below which noise does not negatively affect us. Secondly, we must attempt to differentiate more precisely the two systems of sound pickup and try to enhance and utilize those special qualities of sound reception which are associated with the acupuncture system. This is important in therapeutic applications of music and must also of course play a role in the total musical experience.

## MUSIC FOR THE REDUCTION OF PAIN

I frequently use music to alleviate pain. The procedure is best described through the use of the following examples:

I saw a man today who had severely injured his toe. It was very painful. My first step was to determine the meridian affected by the pain. I had him test-touch each of the meridian alarm points (refer to I.E.L.E.C. Chart # 1.) When he test-touched the stomach meridian alarm point he tested weak, indicating that the stomach meridian on the affected side was the meridian of involvement. Now all that was required to alleviate the pain was to apply music to the two points related to the stomach meridian. These are called the first tonification point and the association point and are marked on the chart.* As well, sound was also applied to the thymus because the thymus is a master controller of the meridian system. The sound was

* This is a musical modification of Dr. George Goodheart's tapping technique. Later research would seem to indicate that application of the sound directly to the meridian test points is equally as effective. Refer to Chart #1 for diagram of test points.

introduced by using special audio transducers.* One was applied to each of the three points and appropriate music and sounds (a Biological Harmonics tape) was directed into the points for a few minutes.

The patient then found that the pain was greatly relieved, and even when his toe was squeezed he could tolerate it. He stated that he now felt quite comfortable and was able to put on his shoe and walk for the first time since the injury. The cause of the pain still persisted but the pain itself had been all but eradicated.

I saw another man who had been in a serious accident the previous day in which he had sustained four broken ribs. He was in considerable pain. It will be found that several meridians will be involved in a large area. To determine them I gently palpated the traumatized region, feeling for any areas of pain. Then I activated the pain to reveal the meridian which was involved with that particular small area. This pain was relieved with the music. We then moved on to another area and continued until all had been cleared.

The procedure took about fifteen minutes. The patient remarked that about 80% of his pain was gone and he was able to breathe and move much more freely. The pain did recur, although much less severely, a few hours later and at that time the procedure was repeated. After that, he stated that he did not require any help with

* called "Master Sound," these are available from Scientific Innovators International, Inc., Aiken, SC 29801.

the minor discomfort that remained. Again I must point out that the pathological process, the fractures, were not healed, but the pain had been greatly reduced.

## *DENTAL ANALGESIA AND ANESTHESIA*

I use a similar procedure for dental analgesia and anesthesia. I have used music as the sole anesthesia for dental extractions and on many occasions have used it for the relief of toothache. It can also be used as an adjunct to routine local anesthesia for dental extractions. In these cases both the patients and the dentists report that there is much less stress and bleeding and less post-operative pain and discomfort. As I have stated, music has also been used as the sole anesthesia, sometimes in most difficult extractions. As with acupuncture anesthesia, it is probable that only certain people are suitable for it and it may not be suitable for all as the sole anesthetic agent, but as an adjunct it has tremendous value in virtually all cases.

The procedure is as follows: by an examination of Chart # 1 you can readily determine the meridian associated with each tooth. Suppose the third lower molar is to be removed. You can see that this will involve the kidney meridian on the particular side. Before the extraction is to commence, the three transducers are placed in position. We ask the patient to hold one over his thymus. The one over the association point on the back usually will be held in place by the weight of the patient's body, and the "musical anesthesiologist" or the dentist himself applies the third transducer to the appropriate point. Then selected therapeutic music is played through the transducers.* This should begin several minutes prior to the commencement of the procedure and continues preferably a few minutes after the procedure is completed.

It is important that the patient be able to hear the music as well. It will be found that pain will be reduced when there is deep rhythmic breathing. And conversely, when pain is experienced the breath will be shallow and irregular. The music is selected particularly to encourage deep regular breathing, and through this the patient's pain will be reduced via the ears as well as via the acupuncture system where it has been directly applied.

It will also be found that by listening to the tapes the dentist will be less stressed himself.

To ensure that the breathing remains regular, the "musical anesthesiologist" pays close attention to the patient's breathing. If he notices the patient is jamming his breath, he gives a prearranged signal – for example, tapping his hand, to remind him to breathe freely.

– – – – –

* We have designed the Biological Harmonics series of tapes for a number of applications, of which this is one. Each tape contains very carefully selected passages of high energy music plus specific biological sounds which aid in stress reduction. Deep regular breathing is facilitated through the use of these tapes.

Pain seems to be a jamming or a buildup of acupuncture energy in a specific meridian or several meridians. Music appears to encourage the flow of energy through the meridian preventing and overcoming the buildup of this energy. Regular breathing will have the same effect. Thus I have found on many occasions that whenever someone is in pain just getting him to breathe deeply and rhythmically will lessen the pain. And of course music can be of great benefit in this regard. As the distressed baby is relieved when his mother holds him in her arms and rocks him and sings to him, so music can comfort us.

The uses of music in medicine are myriad. The results in pain reduction have been most beneficial. From these and other examples we can see that music seems to have two primary modes of action – a direct effect on the acupuncture energy system probably via specific acupuncture points on the skin, and also its central effects for example on respiration. And then of course there are the more obvious attributes of music of which we are so aware, its passion and beauty and spirituality. The wonders of music and its benefits to mankind are endless.

# SUMMARY OF SOME FINDINGS CONCERNING MUSIC AND SOUND

1. All sounds have a definite and demonstrable effect on our life energy.

2. All natural unstressed sounds will raise life energy. This includes the sounds of animals, the sounds of musical instruments, and the biological sounds of the body, particularly the breath sounds and heart sounds. However, when the animal is in distress or when the human body is diseased the sounds may lower life energy.

3. All noise, regardless of its volume, will have a negative effect on life energy. All perfectly regular sounds will have a negative effect – for example, the ticking of a clock or a metronome. Nothing we hear in nature is exactly regular so when we hear artificial regularity it is perceived as a stress and we respond accordingly.

4. All music (except some rock "music") raises life energy and reduces stress. The degree of enhancement is dependent on the life energies of the composer and of the performer. Some of the therapeutic properties are directly related to the composer and are inherent in the music per se and are irrespective of the performer, whereas others are dependent on the performer.

5. Electronically originated sounds such as synthesizer music will be neither energy enhancing nor energy reducing. It is neutral.

6. There are two separate systems of hearing, the obvious system via the ear, and the acupuncture system of the body. The effects of the latter are only apparent with low frequencies (up to approximately 1,000 Hz.). As well, the body responds to frequencies well above the audible threshold (approximately 50 KHz.).

7. Each acupuncture meridian responds to specific frequencies and specific tempi of the metronome. Each meridian relates to a specific gesture and to the gestures involved when playing an instrument as well as dance gestures. Each meridian responds to a particular consonant (whereas the vowels relate to the thymus, a controller of the acupuncture meridian system).

Most importantly each meridian relates to a specific emotional state.* Thus it is that certain sounds and gestures will have particular effects on our emotional state, not only because of what is heard through the ear, but also by activating the specific meridian and thus its associated emotional state.

8. Music is primarily a property of the right cerebral hemisphere. Whenever an individual is stressed an imbalance is introduced between the two hemispheres so that one hemisphere now becomes dominant, and when there is hemisphere imbalance there is diminished creativity. In the case of left-brain dominance this is restored by thinking of music – thus the extremely important role of

---

* See LIFE ENERGY: Understanding and Transforming Your Emotions to Achieve Total Health.

music in our left-brain-dominant society. It corrects the left brain predominance that the stress of our daily living has introduced, rebalancing the hemispheres and thus enabling us to be relaxed, unstressed and creative.

9. Speech is a function of both hemispheres. The left hemisphere is primarily concerned with semantics and the right with syntax, rhythm, rhyme and gesture. In most people there is an imbalance between the hemispheres such that their own internal speech (their thoughts) can actually lower their life energy.

10. The basic purpose of all human communication is to raise the life energy of the listener. There are a number of levels of energy of human communication, ranging from "decidedly untherapeutic" to "transcendental."

11. There are measurable levels of energy for every performer and composer throughout his life. These can be delineated through testing. Further, through implementation of certain recommendations it is possible to raise the life energy of both performers and composers so that their communications have less stress and higher life energy and thus can be of greater benefit to the listener.

12. The group dynamics of performance can be studied to reveal the interplay between conductor and orchestral players and between members of chamber music groups.

13. The majority of professional musicians no longer love their instruments nor music. Music for them has become a stress. These negative effects are reversible.

## TOWARDS AN UNDERSTANDING OF BEETHOVEN: SOME PRELIMINARY NOTES

*"Music is the mediator between the spiritual and the sensual life."* – *Beethoven*

This is intended as a brief communication to delineate some of our findings concerning Beethoven and his music. It is not intended in any way to be comprehensive or complete. It is offered rather as a stimulus for thought.

In the Biological Harmonics research program of the Institutes we have found that with nearly all composers there is a progressive increase in the life energy of their compositions over their creative life spans, and Beethoven is an example of this. At times however we find that there has been an abrupt reduction in life energy. This is uncommon, but the instances are important – for example, Mozart, Sibelius and Schoenberg to name just three. But generally there is on testing an increase in energy from the earliest works to those of old age. In some instances a rise in the level of energy can be attributed to a specific event in the life history of the composer, but usually this is not the case. With Beethoven there are some clues that may explain increases at certain times with certain compositions. It may be that if we knew his biographical data thoroughly enough we would find psychological reasons behind each increase in energy. Be that as it may, the interpretations that are offered are merely suggestions requiring much more research.

Please bear in mind that the testing procedures used to arrive at the conclusions which I will present are far more complex than the general testing techniques as described in this book. The primary reason for this is that Beethoven's life energy in his compositions is so high even in his earliest works that far deeper levels of testing must be employed to ascertain the limits of the life energy in his communications.

– – – – –

Every composer has what we call a basic meridian of communication. This is his symbolic gesture in music. It is to strengthen this meridian that the musical communication is created. In Beethoven's case the basic meridian of communication is the kidney meridian; that is to say all his musical communications were his attempts to correct this basic imbalance within himself. And we find that gradually throughout his life, as he progressively reaches new levels of life energy, there are corresponding new levels of correction of this basic kidney meridian weakness.

Every meridian weakness has an associated negative emotional attitude.* Thus by determining the basic meridian of communication we know the basic emotional drive that led Beethoven into music and which he tried to correct through his compositions. The basic negative attitude, which will come as no surprise to those acquainted with Beethoven's biographical data,+ is that of sexual indecision.

We see this particular meridian imbalance for example in a patient who cannot make up his mind as to with which person he should have sexual relations, or whether he should have them at all, or whether he should have them with someone of his own sex. The literature concerning Beethoven is replete with suggestions concerning his sexual problems, and even what has been termed his latent homosexuality. (His sexual indecision has now been confirmed by our testing.) This kidney meridian weakness is even present in his earliest composition that we have tested, a song he wrote in 1783 at the age of twelve or thirteen.

Beethoven's energy from his earliest compositions remains constant at this level (A) until about the time of the Heiligenstadt Testament of 1802. Thus we find the First Symphony, written in 1800, and Op. 28, written in 1801, are of lower energy than the Op. 31 piano sonatas which are recognized by most authorities as revealing a heightening of his powers.

---

* refer to LIFE ENERGY: Understanding and Transforming Your Emotions to Achieve Total Health.

\+ I highly recommend BEETHOVEN by Maynard Solomon, New York, 1977.

This higher level (B) continues through the Second Symphony (1802) and the Third (1803) and the Fourth (1806), and on until nearly the end of the third movement of the Fifth Symphony. This next level (C) is maintained in the Sixth Symphony, which was worked on almost simultaneously, being completed in late summer in 1808. There is another increase in life energy (level D) which is first manifest with the Choral Fantasy (Op. 80) which was completed in late 1808, and this level is continued until after the Seventh Symphony in 1812.

Let me pause a moment here to discuss one problem with considering these levels. Of course I recognize that a work may have been incubating in Beethoven's mind for a long period of time, perhaps many years, before he finally sat down to the formal task of composition. And thus it is certainly open to question whether one can be specific about levels in view of the length of time that a work has actually been incubating. Be that as it may, it is significant that we do find these changes of energy at these particular times and that all other works written at the same time which I have not delineated in this paper will also have the same energy levels. Further I have found that in every case in which we have tested Beethoven's rejected sketches they have been of much lower energy than the final ones chosen. (His judgment in this was incredibly accurate.) This would also seem to indicate that it was only at the very last stages of composition that the determiner of the energy level, the pulse, was finally injected into the music.

There is a new level of energy (level E) with the Eighth Symphony, or actually in the work that it just preceded – WOO 39 (1812). It is to be noted that the summer of 1812 was the time of the very important "Immortal Beloved" letter and his journey to Linz. This level of activity persists from 1812 to the autumn of 1814 with Op. 90.

There is a period between these dates when it is said that his creativity stopped. This may be so, but we have not been able to determine the energy levels of the few compositions written in that time because we have been unable to obtain suitable performances for testing.

There is another slight rise in energy (level F) with the Elegaic Song, Op. 118, also composed in 1814, and then another rise (level G) in 1815 to 1816 with the Calm Seas and Prosperous Journey, the Cello Sonatas Op. 102, An die ferne Geliebte, the piano sonata Op. 101. This rise in energy may have been triggered by the death of his brother Carl in 1815.

The Hammerklavier Sonata Op. 106 and the piano sonata Op. 109 which was completed in late summer 1820, are at a higher level of energy again (level H). During this time he was in poor physical health, mentally disturbed, and engaged in vicious litigation with Carl's widow Johanna over the custody of his nephew Karl. This was the time of the maximum intensity of his love/hate relationship with Johanna – the hate was apparent, the love implicit.

From 1820 on, there is a change in Beethoven. There is now a complete absence of female friends in his immediate group. There is increased interest in prostitutes (whom he called "fortresses") and a great deal of what any psychiatrist would call latent homosexuality.* This in fact may have been related to the jaundice which was first noticed at this time. Now in many cases of serious liver disease in males there is frequently a diminution of libido and an accentuation of female characteristics; for example, the penis and testicles may shrink in size and the breasts may enlarge. There may even appear on the skin what are called "spider naevi" – small blood vessels of the type of those of the uterus. All of this is in response to their elevated levels of female hormones. Every male produces female hormones which are normally broken down in the liver, but when liver activity is impaired, these hormones build up in the body, leading to an accentuation of female characteristics. It may be that Beethoven's great surge in creativity from this point until the end of his life, and with it the increased high level of the energy of his communications, is at least in part a result of his underlying sexual indecision (his kidney meridian problem) being "resolved" by the hormonal consequences of the liver impairment.

This level (I) is revealed by Op. 110, Op. 111, the Missa Solemnis, the Consecration of the House Overture, the Diabelli Variations, the Bagatelles of Op. 119 and the Ninth Symphony. This further increase of life energy indicates a further resolution of stress within him, particularly of his basic sexual indecision.

Most of the fourth movement of the Ninth Symphony is at an even higher level (J) of energy. I believe it

* e.g., his friends offering to lend him their wives.

is significant that in January of 1824 there was a reconciliation with Johanna. This level of energy occurs at about the time he injected the pulse into the fourth movement – the Ode to Joy (completed February 1824). This level is continued through the Bagatelles Op. 126 and the String Quartets 127, 130 and 132. It is usually recognized by musicologists that he has now a new and simpler style, that his music now reaches back to Bach.*

His last and greatest level (K) is the Grosse Fuge, Op. 131 and Op. 135 and also the transcription of the Grosse Fuge written for four hands (Op. 134) and the new finale for Op. 130, written in October-November 1826.

With these last works Beethoven had reached a very high level of energy. In our testing we have not found a composer who has reached a higher level of energy and it may be that none will – perhaps this is as high a level as a composer can attain. Perhaps the levels higher than this will not be expressed through music but only through silence.

In these last levels no evidence remains of his previous kidney meridian problem. It appears as if he has completely resolved the basic conflict which had disturbed him since childhood and which drove him into music and into composition.

As we can see from the brief biographical data, at

* refer to "Women, Music and Time" in this collection.

least several of his episodes of increased creativity and increased life energy have been influenced by his relationships with women, particularly the Immortal Beloved and Johanna. This I tentatively suggest as evidence in the upsurge of energy when he finally resolves his violent and hateful relationship with Johanna and is reconciled with her at the time he is injecting the pulse into the Ode to Joy. And furthermore we learn from Solomon that at the time of his death it was Johanna who was with him and to whom he indirectly willed his belongings. In his last works he triumphed over his basic sexual indecision. He was now free and clear. He had finally, through his music, resolved the deepest torment of his life.

The problem that Beethoven solved for himself is a problem that to some extent or other torments us all. It deals with the basic relationship of our love for our parents. When we open ourselves to Beethoven the problem is solved for us as it was, albeit tragically, for him. This is his gift to mankind.

## THE IDEAL CONCERT

My most fervent desire for music is the following:

a composer of the highest energy who has long ago surmounted all the imbalances that first led him into composition. He has now reached a rarefied plateau which had never been reached before. He is totally free and charged only with the highest positive emotional attitudes;

his work performed by a conductor of the highest energy and orchestra of the highest energy who are dedicated to the transmission of this most healing of all prayers to the world – totally committed to raising their life energy to the highest state possible for the good of themselves and everyone, pulsing with vibrant life energy, devoted to the communion of the message of love;

an audience which above all else desires and cherishes this message and reveres it for what it is – a manifestation of God on earth.

All this is possible.

Beyond the music waits the silence.

APPENDIX I

## THE STANDARD DELTOID TEST

The testing involves two people, the test subject and the tester. To perform the standard test "in the clear," do the following:

1. Have the subject stand erect, right arm relaxed at his side, left arm held out straight from the side and parallel to the floor, elbow straight.*

2. Face the subject and place your left hand on his right shoulder to steady him. Then place your right hand on the subject's extended left arm just above the wrist.

3. Tell the subject you are going to try to push his arm down as he resists with all his strength.

4. Now push down on his arm fairly quickly, firmly and evenly. The idea is to push just hard enough to test the spring and bounce in the arm, not so hard that the muscle becomes fatigued. It is not a question of who is stronger, but of whether the muscle can "lock" the shoulder joint against the push.

   Note: Do not smile when you are conducting a test or are being tested yourself.

If the subject is able to resist the pressure, we say he tests strong – that is, he is not adversely affected by the test stimulus. If he is unable to resist, we say he tests weak – his life energy has been adversely affected by the test stimulus.

For full directions, see YOUR BODY DOESN'T LIE.

---

* You may use the other arm if you wish.

APPENDIX II

## THE THYMUS TEST

To perform the thymus test, follow this general procedure:

1. Test your subject in the clear, using the standard deltoid test.

2. Have your subject place the fingertips of his free hand on the skin over the point where the second rib joins the breastbone (the manubriosternal joint). This point is directly over the thymus gland.

3. With your subject touching the thymus point, test the indicator muscle again. If he tests strong, his thymus gland (and hence his life energy) is not adversely affected by the stimulus; if he tests weak, then he is adversely affected.

For full directions, see YOUR BODY DOESN'T LIE, p. 46.

APPENDIX III

## THE UMBILICUS TEST

To perform the umbilicus test, follow this general procedure:

1. Test your subject in the clear, using the standard deltoid test.

2. Have the subject touch his umbilicus with the fingers of his right hand. He should test strong.

3. Have the subject remove his right hand from his umbilicus, and then with <u>your</u> left hand touch it. He should test strong.

4. Keeping your left hand on the subject's umbilicus, have him put his right hand on your left hand. If he tests weak, we say he has an umbilicus problem. If he tests strong, we say he has a negative umbilicus reaction.

For full directions and explanation, see "The Umbilicus Test," THE COLLECTED PAPERS OF JOHN DIAMOND, VOLUME II.

## ABOUT THE AUTHOR

John Diamond, M.D., practices preventive medicine and psychiatry in Valley Cottage, New York. He graduated cum laude, Sydney University Medical School, and in 1962 was awarded his Diplomate in Psychological Medicine at Melbourne University. He is a fellow and Past President of the International Academy of Preventive Medicine; Director, Archaeus Research Foundation; Consultant, Community Music School, State University of New York; he has held numerous senior clinical and university teaching appointments in clinical psychiatry, basic sciences, and the humanities; has given over 1,000 lectures to professional organizations, radio and television appearances; is co-editor of the monthly Diamond Report; and conducts ongoing research and works with individuals at his Institutes for the Enhancement of Life Energy and Creativity.

One of Dr. Diamond's most consuming interests over the years has been the relationship between music and health. He has conducted research in this field for over twenty-five years and has implemented his findings in his clinical practice, a major segment of which is devoted to the enhancement of creativity and performance and the reduction of stress in amateur and professional musicians. He has lectured widely in America and Europe, including the Salzburg Easter Festival Symposium sponsored by the Herbert von Karajan Foundation. Among his numerous publications are: YOUR BODY DOESN'T LIE; THE LIFE ENERGY IN MUSIC, VOLUMES I & II; THE RE-MOTHERING EXPERIENCE; SPEECH, LANGUAGE, AND THE POWER OF THE BREATH; LECTURES ON A SPIRITUAL BASIS OF HOLISTIC THERAPY; and LIFE ENERGY.